BEGINNERS' FRENCH

An Introduction to Conversational French

French Conversation Series:

Beginners' French—An Introduction to Conversational French
Conversational French—A Course for Adults

German Conversation Series:

Beginners' German—An Introduction to Conversational German
Conversational German—A Course for Adults

Italian Conversation Series (with Ottavio Negro):

Beginners' Italian—An Introduction to Conversational Italian
Conversational Italian—A Course for Adults

BEGINNERS' FRENCH

An Introduction to Conversational French

JOSEPH HARVARD

With illustrations by
PATRICIA ADAMSON

HODDER AND STOUGHTON
LONDON SYDNEY AUCKLAND TORONTO

Tape and cassette recordings of *Beginners' French* are available from
the Tutor-Tape Company Ltd, 2 Replingham Road, London SW18.
They can be inspected at their Central London Demonstration
Room, 102 Great Russell Street, London WC1.

Examples of the French vowel sounds on cassette can be
obtained from Camera Talks, 31 North Row, London W1R 2EN,
also the sequence of filmstrips, *Les Sons du Français*, which will
be of interest to teachers.

ISBN 0 340 08575 4

Thirteenth impression 1980

Printed in Great Britain for Hodder and Stoughton Educational, a
division of Hodder and Stoughton Ltd., Mill Road, Dunton Green,
Sevenoaks, Kent by J W Arrowsmith Ltd, Bristol

PREFACE

This course is based on considerable practical experience in teaching beginners to speak French. It is essential for a student who wishes to learn the conversational language to study it from the very beginning; moreover, as the spoken language is the easiest form of the language, this approach is particularly suitable for all beginners, no matter what their ultimate purpose in learning the language may be.

The ability to speak a language cannot be gained from grammar study or reading, but like any other skill it can be acquired only through systematic and diligent practice. This book provides the material for such practice and presents it in the most suitable way for easy memorising and assimilation.

The lessons in the book have therefore been planned along the following lines. Each lesson begins with a short dialogue which should be thoroughly committed to memory. New words are explained through footnotes on the same page, so that no separate vocabulary is necessary. It will be seen that the great majority of the sentences learnt will serve as models for the formation of numerous other sentences, by the replacement of any word or word-group in the sentence with others of similar structure. This process of substitution is clearly shown in each lesson by the arrangement of several examples of sentence pattern in the form of 'substitution tables'. These combine several interchangeable word-groups and enable the student to form from them a large number of useful sentences. The student should read aloud as many combinations as possible by taking in turn one entry from each column in the table until all have been completely assimilated and each sentence can be immediately recalled. Only then should the exercises at the end of the book be attempted.

This approach to the learning of a language does not exclude the treatment of grammar. However, grammar itself is not language: it is merely information about it, and when presented, as in this book, after the appearance and practice of each new language form it loses the unpleasant aura which it possesses for many students, and becomes a welcome clarification.

5

In the experience of the author, fluency in any foreign language can be achieved only through practice comparable to—and as necessary as—the finger exercises which must be mastered when learning to play the piano. The method followed in this book ensures that correct expressions only are learnt, and enables the student to proceed confidently from the simple French in the present volume to the more complex forms of expression introduced in the subsequent volumes of the series. These are not merely sequels to *Beginners' French* but also companion books for use in conjunction with it. By its very nature, *Beginners' French* can give only a piecemeal introduction to French grammar, but the second book in the series, *Conversational French,* contains a systematic grammar of the spoken language, as well as a number of useful conversations concerned with foreign travel. Other features of the book are classified lists of the more important idioms for everyday conversation and a great number of sentence-building tables for further fluency practice.

The study of his textbooks will give a student a good basic knowledge of the rudiments of the language. As soon as possible, however, he should start reading some *real* French, i.e., texts written for the enjoyment of French people. The easiest texts, and the most useful from the point of view of the student of the spoken language, are to be found in modern plays and in the dialogues of films. In order to provide a selection of such material a companion book to this course, *French for Pleasure,* has been compiled. Many of the items selected are easy enough for a student to read during his first year of study.

A full explanation of the author's methods and practical advice in the use of the course are given in his *Teaching Adults to Speak a Foreign Language,* which also serves as a Teacher's Book to the series.

In conclusion, the author is greatly indebted to Miss P. Adamson, of Camera Talks, for her charming illustrations and to Mr. R. S. Kirkman, of the University of London Press Ltd, for his valuable assistance in the preparation of this course.

J.H.

CONTENTS

SPEECH SOUNDS

French pronunciation cannot be learned from a book. Those who learn without a teacher or do not have the help of a French-speaking person should obtain the tapes or the gramophone record issued in conjunction with this course.[1] These aids are almost as important for those who also attend classes. As adult classes usually meet only once a week the teacher's pronunciation will only be vaguely remembered when the students read over their lessons at home and the beginner, reading them without such aids, is bound to acquire a wrong pronunciation, which once ingrained will be most difficult to unlearn!

Nor is it possible for most adults to learn French pronunciation through imitation alone. For some of the sounds it is necessary to know the position of lips and jaws, and whether the sounds are made at the front or the back of the mouth. Students attending classes will receive this information from their teacher. The following notes are chiefly intended for those who learn without a teacher, and should be studied only with the help of a French-speaking person or one of the recordings mentioned on page 4.

VOWELS

French vowels are pure vowel sounds, which means that lips, jaw and tongue remain in the same position throughout whilst the sound is uttered. This has to be constantly borne in mind when consulting the following table, as the nearest English equivalent given does not have quite the same sound. Most English vowels are not pure sounds but diphthongs: e.g., the *o* in home is pronounced as a mixture of two sounds, something like h*o-e*m. The learner has to beware of this and realise that the vowel sounds in the French words *Gaulle, père* and *dé* are not quite the same as those in the English words goal, pair and day.

There are 16 vowel sounds, which are best learned in four groups. A beginner should first learn to associate each sound with its normal spelling and later with the various alternative spellings shown on pages 90 and 91.

[1] see page 4.

9

I. Front Vowels

These are produced in the front part of the mouth. The mouth is almost closed for No. 1, remains so for No. 2, is nearly half open for No. 3 and a little wider for No. 4. The corners of the mouth are wide apart for No. 1, only slightly less so for No. 2, and in normal position for Nos. 3 and 4. When saying the four sounds in succession the mouth gradually opens and the corners of the mouth become less far apart.

SOUND	NEAREST ENGLISH EQUIVALENT	EXAMPLES	
No. 1	*i* in *machine*	le lit, *bed* la pipe, *pipe*	le nid, *nest* vide, *empty*
No. 2	*a* in *taste*	le thé, *tea* le bébé, *baby*	la clé, *key* l'été, *summer*
No. 3	*e* in *get*	le lait, *milk* le nègre, *negro*	la fraise, *strawberry* la chèvre, *goat*
No. 4	halfway between *a* in *cat* and *cart*	le chat, *cat* le canard, *duck*	la vache, *cow* madame

II. Back Vowels

These are produced at the back of the mouth. For No. 5 the mouth is opened still wider than for No. 4, i.e., as when the doctor tells us to say 'ah'. For Nos. 6 to 8, the mouth gradually closes, whilst the lips are more and more rounded.

SOUND	NEAREST ENGLISH EQUIVALENT	EXAMPLES	
No. 5	*a* in *father*	l'âne, *donkey* le château, *castle*	le gâteau, *cake* la tasse, *cup*
No. 6	*o* in *not*	la pomme, *apple* la cloche, *bell*	le coq, *rooster* l'homme, *man*
No. 7	*o* in *note*	le dôme, *dome* la rose, *rose*	le veau, *calf* l'auto, *car*
No. 8	*oo* in *root*	la roue, *wheel* le chou, *cabbage*	la poule, *hen* fou, *mad*

III. Mixed Vowels

These are front vowels produced with the lips in the same position as for back vowels, i.e., completely rounded for No. 9, a little less for No. 10 and only slightly rounded for Nos. 11 and 12.

SOUND	NEAREST ENGLISH EQUIVALENT	EXAMPLES	
No. 9	*ea* as in *lean* with lips rounded	la lune, *moon* la mule, *mule*	le mur, *wall* la flûte, *flute*
No. 10	*ay* in *day* with lips rounded	deux, *two* la queue, *tail*	le feu, *fire* il pleut, *it rains*
No. 11	*u* in curtain with lips slightly rounded	l'œuf, *egg* le cœur, *heart*	le bœuf, *ox* les fleurs, *flowers*
No. 12	*e* in open with lips slightly rounded	le repas, *meal* la devise, *motto, slogan*	le repos, *rest* le secret, *secret*

IV. Nasal Vowels

These are produced by saying the corresponding non-nasal vowel (indicated in brackets) breathing out through both nose and mouth.

SOUND	NEAREST ENGLISH EQUIVALENT	EXAMPLES	
No. 13 (No. 6)	The vowel sound in *long*	le pont, *bridge* le cochon, *pig*	la pompe, *pump* le mouton, *sheep*
No. 14 (No. 5)	The vowel sound in *arm*	le banc, *seat* la tente, *tent*	le champ, *field* le vent, *wind*
No. 15 (No. 3)	The vowel sound in *hang*	le singe, *monkey* le timbre, *stamp* le bain, *bath*	la dinde, *turkey* le train, *train*
No. 16 (No. 11)	The vowel sound in *earn*	un, *one* le parfum, *perfume*	Verdun, Melun *(names of towns)*

V. Diphthongs: These are combinations of vowels and sounds similar to English *w* (as in *was*) and *y* (as in *yes*).

SPELLING	NEAREST ENGLISH EQUIVALENT	EXAMPLES
oi[1]	The part in heavy type of '**w**as' quickly followed by sound No. 5	une étoile, *star* la poire, *pear* une armoire, *cupboard*
ui	Sound No. 9 quickly followed by sound No. 1	la nuit, *night* le puits, *well* la pluie, *rain*
ou followed by another vowel	**w** quickly pronounced with the following vowel	oui, *yes* ouest, *west* le pingouin, *penguin*
i ⎱ followed by *y* ⎰ a vowel	**y** as in yes	le pied, *foot* le soulier, *shoe* les yeux, *eyes*
ill	The parts in heavy type of 's**ee yes**'[2]	la fille, *daughter* la papillon, *butterfly* la cuillère, *spoon*
ail ⎱ *aill* ⎰	The parts in heavy type of '**ah yes**'	le travail, *work* les rails, *rails* le tailleur, *tailor*
eil ⎱ *eille* ⎰ *ay*	The parts in heavy type of 'g**ay yes**'[3]	le soleil, *sun* la bouteille, *bottle* payer, *to pay*
euil ⎱ *œil* ⎰ *euill*	The parts in heavy type of 's**ir yes**'	le fauteuil, *easy chair* l'œil, *eye* la feuille, *leaf*
ouill	The parts in heavy type of 'y**ou yes**'	la grenouille, *frog* bouillir, *to boil*

[1] *also* oe *in* la poêle *(frying pan)*, le poêle *(stove)*, la moelle *(marrow) and* o *in the combination* oy, *e.g.* le moyen *(means)*, loyal, royal.

[2] *but not in words beginning with* ill-, *e.g.* illustration, *nor in* la ville, la villa, le village, mille, million, millimètre, distiller, Lille, tranquille.

[3] *but like* '**ah y**(es)' *in* Bayard, Biscaye, Bayonne, Mayence, La Fayette, *and a few others.*

CONSONANTS

All French consonant sounds are pronounced clearly, but with less force than their English equivalents. There should be no breath between a consonant and its following vowel. A good way to practise this is to hold a lighted match in front of your mouth while saying *Paris*. When you say it in English the light will certainly flicker or even go out, because there is quite a lot of breath coming out of your mouth. When you can say *Paris* in such a way that the flame remains undisturbed, you will have obtained the correct French *p* sound. The same applies to *b, m, f,* and *v,* which like *p* are produced by separating the lips. Use less force than in English and let as little air as possible escape from your mouth while making these sounds. The pronunciation of the various consonants is explained on pages 92 ff.

STRESS

French pronunciation differs from English in other ways besides the quality of individual sounds. Take for instance the word *général,* which is common to both languages. In the English pronunciation of this word a heavy stress is put on the first syllable, whereas the others are mumbled or even completely slurred together. Although the word has three syllables, it often sounds as though it has only one. In the French word *général,* on the other hand, each syllable must be given equal prominence. French speech is like a string of pearls which are all of the same size whilst English may be likened to a string of beads where big beads alternate with several small ones.

INTONATION

A further difference between French and English speech is that the voice does not rise and fall in the same way in the two languages. The different intonations of the two languages may be compared to different tunes, and it is not much more difficult to acquire the correct French intonation than it is to learn a new tune. Just as it is so much easier to learn a tune by ear and imitation, the intonation of a foreign language can best be learned by hearing natives talk and trying to imitate the different way in which the voice rises and falls in their language.

THE ALPHABET

LETTER	FRENCH NAME AND PRONUNCIATION	LETTER	FRENCH NAME AND PRONUNCIATION
a	*a*	n	*enne*
b	*bé*	o	*o*
c	*cé*	p	*pé*
d	*dé*	q	*ku*
e	*e*	r	*erre*
f	*effe*	s	*esse*
g	*gé*	t	*té*
h	*ache*	u	*u*
i	*i*	v	*vé*
j	*ji*	w	*double vé*
k	*ka*	x	*iks*
l	*elle*	y	*i grec*
m	*emme*	z	*zède*

SIGNS AND ACCENTS

1. *Accent Aigu* (ˊ) is used over *e* only to indicate the closed sound, e.g. *le thé, l'été, aimé.*

2. *Accent Grave* (ˋ) placed over *e* indicates the open sound, e.g. *le père, la mère, j'amène.*

Over *a* and *u* it does not indicate any difference in pronunciation, but distinguishes meanings, e.g. *a* (has) from *à* (to); *ou* (or) from *où* (where).

3. *Accent Circonflexe* (ˆ) indicates that the vowel is long, e.g. *la fenêtre, l'île, la côte.*

4. *La Cédille* (ˌ) is placed under *c* to show that it is pronounced like sharp *s*, and not like *k*, before *a, o, u*, e.g. *leçon, français, reçu.*

5. *Le Tréma* (¨) indicates that the vowel bearing it is pronounced separately from the vowel preceding it, e.g. *Noël, naïf, haïr.*

6. *L'Apostrophe* (ˈ) indicates omission of a vowel, e.g. *l'ami, s'il vient, jusqu'ici.*

NUMERALS

	CARDINAL		ORDINAL
1	un, une	1st	le premier, la première
2	deux	2nd	le second, la seconde
3	trois		le deuxième, la deuxième
4	quatre	3rd	le (la) troisième
5	cinq	4th	le (la) quatrième
6	six	5th	le (la) cinquième
7	sept	6th	le (la) sixième
8	huit	7th	le (la) septième
9	neuf	8th	le (la) huitième
10	dix	9th	le (la) neuvième
11	onze	10th	le (la) dixième
12	douze	11th	le (la) onzième
13	treize	12th	le (la) douzième
14	quatorze	13th	le (la) treizième
15	quinze	14th	le (la) quatorzième
16	seize	15th	le (la) quinzième
17	dix-sept	16th	le (la) seizième
18	dix-huit	17th	le (la) dix-septième
19	dix-neuf	18th	le (la) dix-huitième
20	vingt	19th	le (la) dix-neuvième
21	vingt et un	20th	le (la) vingtième
22	vingt-deux	21st	le (la) vingt et unième
23	vingt-trois	22nd	le (la) vingt-deuxième
30	trente	100th	le (la) centième
31	trente et un	1,000th	le (la) millième
32	trente-deux		
40	quarante		
50	cinquante		
60	soixante		
70	soixante-dix		
71	soixante et onze		
72	soixante-douze		
73	soixante-treize		

79	soixante-dix-neuf	110	cent dix
80	quatre vingts	200	deux cents
81	quatre-vingt-un	1,000	mille
90	quatre-vingt-dix	1,500	mille cinq cents
91	quatre-vingt-onze	2,000	deux mille
99	quatre-vingt-dix-neuf	10,000	dix mille
100	cent	100,000	cent mille
101	cent un	1,000,000	un million

FRACTIONS

$\frac{1}{2}$	une moitié
$\frac{1}{3}$	un tiers
$\frac{1}{4}$	un quart
$\frac{1}{5}$, etc.	un cinquième, *etc.*, *ending in* -ième
$\frac{3}{4}$	trois quarts
$\frac{7}{8}$	sept huitièmes
$3\frac{1}{2}$	trois et demi

The words expressing fractions are nouns: *la moitié d'un pain*, half a loaf.

Demi is the adjective corresponding to *la moitié*; it agrees when it follows a noun: *midi et demi, une heure et demie*. Before a noun *demi* is invariable: *une demi-heure*.

Leçon Un

Entrez!

Prenez place!

Fumez-vous?

Je ne fume pas.

Ne fumez pas!

N'entrez pas!

ICI ON PARLE FRANÇAIS

A : *Un homme.*   B : *Une dame.*

A : Bonjour, madame (mademoiselle).

B : Bonjour, monsieur.

A : Entrez,* s'il vous plaît.[1] Prenez place.*

B : Merci.

A : Vous parlez français, n'est-ce pas?[2]

B : Très[3] peu.[4] Ne parlez-vous pas[F] anglais?[5]

A : Pas[E] très bien.[6] Fumez-vous,* madame?

B : Merci. Je ne fume pas.*

---

[1] s'il vous plaît, *please (lit. 'if it pleases you')*.
[2] n'est-ce pas? *is short for* n'est-ce pas vrai? *'isn't it true?' It is the French equivalent for 'don't you?' 'isn't it?' 'aren't you?' etc.*
[3] *very.*
[4] *little.*
[5] *English.*
[6] *well.*

ABBREVIATIONS used throughout the lessons:

* : *see Illustrations.*	m.: *masculine.*	fam.: *familiar.*
F : *see Fluency Practice.*	f.: *feminine.*	lit.: *literally.*
E : *see Explanations.*	pl.: *plural.*	

FLUENCY PRACTICE

1. | | |
    |---|---|
    | Entrez! | *Come (or go) in!* |
    | Montez! | *Come (or go) up!* |
    | Regardez! | *Look!* |
    | Écoutez! | *Listen!* |
    | Parlez français! | *Speak French!* |

2. | | |
    |---|---|
    | N'entrez pas! | *Don't* \| *come (or go) in!* |
    | Ne montez pas! | *come (or go) up!* |
    | Ne regardez pas! | *look!* |
    | N'écoutez pas! | *listen!* |
    | Ne parlez pas si vite! | *speak so fast!* |

3. Vous | entrez, | n'est-ce pas?   *You are* | *coming (going) in,* | *aren't you?*
    montez,   *coming (going) up,*
    regardez,   *looking,*
    écoutez,   *listening,*
    parlez anglais,   *You speak English, don't you?*

18

4.	Vous	n'entrez pas?	*You are not*	*coming (going) in?*
		ne montez pas?		*coming (going) up?*
		ne regardez pas?		*looking?*
		n'écoutez pas?		*listening?*
		ne parlez pas français?	*You don't speak French?*	

5.	Entrez-vous?	*Are you*	*coming (going) in?*
	Montez-vous?		*coming (going) up?*
	Regardez-vous?		*looking?*
	Écoutez-vous?		*listening?*
	Parlez-vous espagnol?	*Do you speak Spanish?*	

6.	N'entrez-vous pas?	*Aren't you*	*coming (going) in?*
	Ne montez-vous pas?		*coming (going) up?*
	Ne regardez-vous pas?		*looking?*
	N'écoutez-vous pas?		*listening?*
	Ne parlez-vous pas anglais?	*Don't you speak English?*	

7.	Oui,	j'entre.	*Yes,*	*I am*	*coming (going) in.*
	Si,[1]	je monte.			*coming (going) up.*
		je regarde.			*looking.*
		j'écoute.			*listening.*
		je parle espagnol.	*Yes, I speak Spanish.*		

[1] *In answer to negative question.*

8.	Non,	je n'entre	pas.	*No, I am not*	*coming (going) in.*
		je ne monte			*coming (going) up.*
		je ne regarde			*looking.*
		je n'écoute			*listening.*
		je ne le parle		*No, I don't speak it.*	

EXPLANATIONS

1. The imperative of verbs (expressing a command or request) ends in *-ez* (pronounced like *é*).

2. The form of the verb used in connection with *vous* ('you') in the present tense is the same as the imperative ending in *-ez*.

3. In connection with *je* (*j'* before a vowel or *h* mute) most verbs in the present tense end in *-e*. This *e* is silent.

4. No difference is made in French between 'I speak' and 'I am speaking'. Both are expressed by *je parle*.

5. The negative of verbs is expressed by *ne . . . pas*. *Ne* (*n'* before a vowel or *h* mute) precedes the verb and *pas* follows it. When there is no verb, *pas* alone is used.

19

Leçon Deux

Une dame monte l'escalier.

Elle chante.

La dame entre dans le salon.

Elle allume l'électricité.

Elle tourne le bouton de la T.S.F.[1]

Elle danse.

[1] télégraphie sans fil, *wireless, radio.*

Dans[1] un Bar

A : *Un Français.* B : *Un Américain.* C : *Un Anglais.*

B : Vous fumez, monsieur?

C : Merci, je ne fume pas.

B : Et vous, monsieur?

A : Je veux bien.[2] Vous êtes[3] bien aimable.[4] C'est[5] une cigarette anglaise, n'est-ce pas?

B : Non, monsieur, c'est une cigarette américaine.

A : Vous êtes Américain, monsieur?

B : Oui, je suis[6] Américain.

A : Et vous, monsieur, êtes-vous aussi[7] Américain?

C : Non, je ne suis pas Américain. Je suis Anglais. Mais[8] ma femme[9] n'est pas Anglaise. Elle est Écossaise.[10]

A : Elle parle donc[11] anglais avec[12] l'accent écossais?

C : Oui, c'est ça.[13] Elle parle même[14] français avec l'accent écossais.

[1] dans, *in*	[9] ma femme, *my wife.*
[2] je veux bien, *I should like to.*	[10] écossais, écossaise, *Scottish.*
[3] vous êtes, *you are.*	[11] *so, therefore.*
[4] bien aimable, *very kind.*	[12] *with.*
[5] c'est, *it is.*	[13] c'est ça, *that's right (lit. 'it is*
[6] je suis, *I am.*	*that').*
[7] *also.* [8] *but.*	[14] *even.*

Fluency Practice

1.

Un monsieur	entre.	*A gentleman*	*is coming*[1] *in.*
Une dame	monte.	*A lady*	*is coming*[1] *up.*
Une demoiselle	parle.	*A young lady*	*is speaking.*
Un garçon	chante.	*A boy*	*is singing.*
Une fillette	danse.	*A little girl*	*is dancing.*
Un homme	regarde.	*A man*	*is looking.*
Une femme	écoute.	*A woman*	*is listening.*

[1] *or going.*

2.

*Est-ce	un professeur	*Is it*	*a teacher*
C'est	un élève	*It is*	*a pupil* (m.)
Ce n'est pas	une élève	*It is not*	*a pupil* (f.)
	un agent de police		*a policeman*
	une femme de chambre		*a chambermaid*
	une infirmière		*a nurse*
	un douanier		*a customs official*

* *Note that this table contains both statements and questions. Punctuation has therefore been omitted.*

3.

Le monsieur	entre.		The gentleman	is coming[1] in.
La dame	n'entre pas.		The lady	is not coming[1] in.
La demoiselle	monte.		The young lady	is coming[1] up.
Le professeur	ne monte pas.		The teacher	is not coming[1] up.
L'élève	écoute.		The pupil	is listening.
Il	n'écoute pas.		He	is not listening.
Elle	parle.		She	is speaking.
	ne parle pas.			is not speaking.

[1] or going.

4.

Est-ce que	le monsieur	parle?		Is	the gentleman	speaking?
	la dame	chante?			the lady	singing?
	le garçon	joue?			the boy	playing?
	la fillette	danse?			the girl	dancing?

5.

Oui,	il	parle.		Yes,	he	is	speaking.
	elle	chante.			she		singing.
		joue.					playing.
		danse.					dancing.

6.

Non,	il	ne	parle	pas.		No,	he	is not	speaking.
	elle		chante				she		singing.
			joue						playing.
			danse						dancing.

7.

Il	parle	un peu.		He	speaks	a little.
Elle	danse	beaucoup.		She	dances	much.
	chante	trop.			sings	too much.
	travaille	beaucoup trop.			works	far too much.
	joue	très bien.			plays	very well.
		assez bien.				quite well.
		mal.				badly.

8.

Je suis	Français(e).		I am	French.
Vous êtes	Anglais(e).		You are	English.
Il est	Écossais(e).		He is	Scottish.
Elle est	Irlandais(e).		She is	Irish.
	Américain(e).			American.
	Canadien(ne).			Canadian.
Je ne suis pas	Australien(ne).		I am not	Australian.
Vous n'êtes pas	Italien(ne).		You are not	Italian.
Il n'est pas	Espagnol(e).		He is not	Spanish.
Elle n'est pas	Allemand(e).		She is not	German.

Êtes-vous	Français(e)?		Are you	French?
Est-il	Belge?		Is he	Belgian?
Est-elle	Suisse?		Is she	Swiss?

22

1. *Un* = 'a, an', before a masculine noun.
   Une = 'a, an', before a feminine noun.

2. *Le* = 'the', before a masculine noun.
   La = 'the', before a feminine noun.

Both *le* and *la* are reduced to *l'* before a noun commencing with a vowel or *h* mute.

3. The form of verbs expressing what he, she or it does (or is doing) ends in *-e*.[1] This ending is silent.

4. *Est-ce que* . . . ? ('is it that . . . ?') placed in front of a statement turns it into a question.

5. *-e* is added to an adjective when the noun it qualifies is feminine. No change is required if the adjective ends in *-e*, e.g. *rouge*, red. If, however, the masculine ends in *-é*, an additional *-e* is required for the feminine:

   e.g. fatigué, fatiguée, *tired*.

Some adjectives double the final consonant before adding *-e*:

bon, bonne, *good*	gentil, gentille, *nice*
gros, grosse, *big, stout*	sot, sotte, *stupid*
cruel, cruelle, *cruel*	ancien, ancienne, *old*

---

[1] There are other verbs ending in *-t* (or *-d*) when used in connection with *il* or *elle*. These will be introduced later in this course.

Leçon Trois

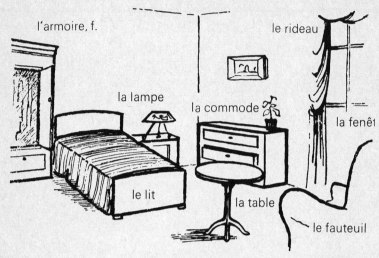

l'armoire, f.

le rideau

la lampe

la commode

la fenê↑

le lit

la table

le fauteuil

LA CHAMBRE

Dans un Hôtel

A : *Le chef de réception.*[1]   ˙B : *Un monsieur.*

B : Avez-vousᶠ une chambre?

A : Nous avonsᶠ une petite chambre avec salle de bains.[2]

B : Quel[3] est le prix[4] de la chambre?

A : Quinze francs par jour,[5] monsieur, et dix pour cent pour le
     service. Voulez-vous[6] voir[7] la chambre?

B : Oui, volontiers.[8]

A : Voulez-vous me suivre,[9] monsieur. Prenons[10] l'ascenseur.[11]

---

[1] le chef de réception, *reception
      clerk.*
[2] la salle de bains, *bathroom.*
[3] *what, which.*
[4] le prix, *price.*
[5] par jour, *per day.*

[6] voulez-vous, *do you wish; will you.*
[7] *to see.*
[8] *gladly.*
[9] *follow.*
[10] *let us take.*
[11] un ascenseur, *lift.*

B : Quel étage?[1]

A : Deuxième,[2] monsieur. Voici[3] la chambre.

B : Elle est très petite. N'avez-vous pas[F] une chambre plus grande?[4]

A : Non, monsieur, pas pour le moment.

B : Très bien.

A : Vous avez un grand lit* très confortable, une petite table, une commode,* un fauteuil* et une grande armoire.* Vous avez aussi le téléphone.

B : Où[5] est la salle de bains?

A : Ici, à côté.[6] A droite[7] vous avez le robinet[8] d'eau[9] chaude[10] et à gauche[11] le robinet d'eau froide.[12]

[1] un étage, *floor.*
[2] *second.*
[3] *here is.*
[4] plus grande, *larger.*
[5] *where.*
[6] à côté, *by the side, next door.*
[7] à droite, *on the right.*
[8] le robinet, *tap.*
[9] l'eau *(f.), water.*
[10] chaud(e), *hot.*
[11] à gauche, *on the left.*
[12] froid(e), *cold.*

FLUENCY PRACTICE

1. La | chambre | est | petite. | *The* | *room* | *is* | *small.*
| table | n'est pas | grande. | | *table* | *is not* | *large.*
| chaise | | | | *chair* | |
ELLE | | | | **IT** | |

2. Le | lit | est | petit. | *The* | *bed* | *is* | *small.*
| fauteuil | n'est pas | grand. | | *armchair* | *is not* | *large.*
| lavabo | | | | *washbasin* | |
IL | | | | **IT** | |

3. Les | chaises | sont | petites. | *The* | *chairs* | *are* | *small.*
| tables | ne sont pas | grandes. | | *tables* | *are not* | *big.*
| chambres | | | | *rooms* | |
ELLES | | | | **THEY** | |

4. Les | lits | sont | petits. | *The* | *beds* | *are* | *small.*
| lavabos | ne sont pas | grands. | *The* | *washbasins* | *are not* | *large.*
| hôtels | | | | *hotels* | |
ILS | | | | **THEY** | |

25

5.	J'ai	une	grande chambre.	I have	a	large room.
	Je n'ai pas		petite table.	I haven't		small table.
	Vous avez		bonne chaise.	You have		good chair.
	Vous n'avez			You haven't		
	pas	un	grand lit.			large bed.
	Il a		petit fauteuil.	He has		small armchair.
	Il n'a pas		bon hôtel.	He·hasn't		good hotel.
	Elle a			She has		
	Elle n'a pas			She hasn't		

6	Est-ce	une	bonne chambre?	Is it	a	good room?
	N'est-ce pas		grande armoire?	Isn't it		large wardrobe?
	Avez-vous		petite valise?	Have you		small suitcase?
	N'avez-vous			Haven't you		
	pas	un	bon lit?			good bed?
	A-t-il		grand hôtel?	Has he		large hotel?
	N'a-t-il pas		petit taxi?	Hasn't he		small taxi?
	A-t-elle			Has she		
	N'a-t-elle			Hasn't she		
	pas					

7.	Nous	fumons.	We are	smoking.
		entrons.		going[1] in.
		montons.		going[1] up.
		mangeons.		eating.

[1] or *coming.*

8.	Fumons.	Let us	smoke.
	Mangeons.		eat.
	Entrons.		go in.
	Montons.		go up.

EXPLANATIONS

1. In grammar 'masculine' and 'feminine' do not mean the same as 'male' and 'female'. In French all nouns (whether names of persons or things) are either masculine or feminine.

2. *Les* = 'the', before any noun in the plural.

3. The plural of most nouns is formed by adding -*s*. This ending is silent.[1]

4. Adjectives also add -*s* in the plural. [1]

[1] If the singular ends in -s, -z or -x there is no change in the plural.

SINGULAR	PLURAL
le fils, *son*	les fils
le nez, *nose*	les nez
vieux, *old*	vieux

5. *Il* = 'it', when replacing a masculine noun.
   Elle = 'it'. when replacing a feminine noun.
   Ils = 'they', when replacing masculine nouns.
   Elles = 'they', when replacing feminine nouns.

6. In connection with *nous* ('we'), verbs end in *-ons*. The same form of the verb, but omitting *nous*, expresses 'let us . . .'

Leçon Quatre

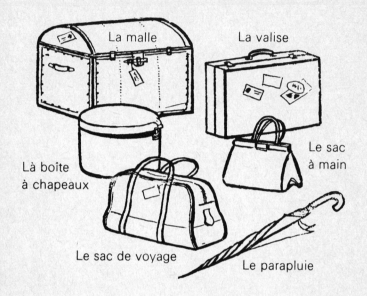

La malle

La valise

Là boîte à chapeaux

Le sac à main

Le sac de voyage

Le parapluie

LES BAGAGES

A : *Un monsieur.* B : *Le garçon d' hôtel.*[1]

A *(au téléphone)* : Faites monter[2] mes bagages, s'il vous plaît.

(Quelques[3] minutes plus tard[4] on frappe[5] à la porte de la chambre No. 12.[6])

A : Entrez!

B : Voici[E] vos bagages, monsieur. Une malle,* deux valises,* et un sac de voyage.* Voici d'abord[7] la malle.

A : Posez-la[E] sur cette chaise devant la fenêtre.

B : Où est-ce que je pose les valises?

[1] *hotel porter.*
[2] faites monter, *have brought up.*
   send up.
[3] *a few.*

[4] plus tard, *later.*
[5] on frappe, *there is a knock.*
[6] numéro douze.
[7] d'abord, *to begin with, first.*

28

A : Posez-les là, derrière le rideau.[1]

B : . . . et le sac de voyage, monsieur?

A : Donnez-le-moi.[E] *(Il le pose sur la table.)*

B : C'est tout,[2] monsieur.

A : Tenez,[3] voilà pour[4] vous. *(Il lui[5] donne[6] un pourboire.[7])*

B : Merci bien, monsieur.

[1] derrière le rideau, *behind the curtain.*
[2] *all.*
[3] *there you are (lit. 'hold').*
[4] *for.*
[5] *(to) him.*
[6] *gives.*
[7] le pourboire, *tip.*

FLUENCY PRACTICE

1.

Les vêtements sont	sur	l'armoire.	*The clothes are*	on	*the wardrobe.*
	sous	la commode.		under	*the chest of drawers.*
	devant			in front of	
Mettez les choses		la malle.	*Put the things*		*the trunk.*
	derrière	la valise.		behind	*the suitcase.*
Mettez-les	à côté de		*Put them*	by the side of	
	dans			in	

2.

Je suis	ici.	*I am*	*here.*
Nous sommes	là.	*We are*	*there.*
Il est	dans le jardin.	*He is*	*in the garden.*
Ils sont	sur le toit.	*They are*	*on the roof.*
Elle est	sous l'arbre.	*She is*	*under the tree.*
Elles sont	devant la maison.	*They are*	*in front of the house.*
Tu es[1]	derrière le garage.	*You are[2]*	*behind the garage.*
Vous êtes	à côté de l'école.	*You are*	*next to the school.*
	près de l'église.		*near the church.*
	loin de la gare.		*far from the station.*

[1] tu *is used when talking to a child or a good friend.* [2] *familiar form.*

3.

Prenez	le parapluie.	*Take*	*the umbrella.*
	-le.		*it (m.).*
	la valise.		*the suitcase.*
	-la.		*it (f.).*
	les choses.		*the things.*
	-les.		*them.*

4.

Mettez-	le	dans	le tiroir.	*Put*	*it (m.).*	*in*	*the drawer.*
	la		l'armoire.		*it (f.)*		*the wardrobe.*
	les		la valise.		*them*		*the suitcase.*

29

5. | Je | le | prends. | | | *I* | *take*[1] | *it* (m.) | |
	la	regarde.				*look at*	*it* (f.)	
	les	ferme.				*shut*	*them*	
		pose.				*put* ..	...	. *down.*
		mets sur la table.				*put* ..	...	. *on the table.*

6. | Il | le | prend. | | | *He* | *takes*[2] | *it* (m.) | |
Elle	la	regarde.			*She*	*looks at*	*it* (f.)	
	les	ouvre.				*opens*	*them*	
		ferme.				*shuts*		
		met dans sa poche.				*puts*..	...	. *into his (her)*
								pocket.

7. | Je | ne | le | touche | pas. | *I* | *don't* | *touch* | *it* (m.).[3] |
Il		la	regarde		*He*	*doesn't*	*look at*	*it* (f.).
Elle		les	garde		*She*		*keep*	*them.*
			ferme				*shut*	

8. | Le | prenez-vous? | | *Do you* | *take* | *it* (m.)?[4] |
| La | gardez-vous? | | | *keep* | *it* (f.)? |
| Les | regardez-vous? | | | *look at* | *them?* |

Ne	le	prenez-vous	pas?	*Don't you*	*take*	*it* (m.)?[5]
	la	gardez-vous			*keep*	*it* (f.)?
	les	regardez-vous			*look at*	*them?*

9. | Ne | le | prenez | pas! | *Don't* | *take* | *it* (m.). |
| | la | fermez | | | *shut* | *it* (f.). |
| | les | gardez | | | *keep* | *them.* |

Ne	le	regardez pas!	*Don't*	*look at*	*him* (or *it*).
	la				*her* (or *it*).
	les				*them.*

10. | J'aime | ce livre-ci. | *I like* | *this book.* |
Je n'aime pas	ce livre-là.	*I don't like*	*that book.*
Je préfère	cette couleur-ci.	*I prefer*	*this colour.*
	cette couleur-là.		*that colour.*

Aimez-vous	ces livres-ci?	*Do you like*	*these books?*
Préférez-vous	ces livres-là?	*Do you prefer*	*those books?*
N'aimez-vous pas	ces couleurs-ci?	*Don't you like*	*these colours?*
Ne préférez-vous pas	ces couleurs-là?	*Don't you prefer*	*those colours?*

[1] or *I am taking, etc.*
[2] or *he is taking, etc.*
[3] or *I am not touching it, etc.*

[4] or *are you taking it? etc.*
[5] or *aren't you taking it? etc.*

1. *Le, la, les,* used in connection with verbs, have different meanings from *le, la, les,* used with nouns.

With verbs, *le* = 'him' *or* 'it' (replacing a masculine noun in the singular),

la = 'her' *or* 'it' (replacing a feminine noun in the singular),

les = 'them' (replacing any noun or nouns in the plural).

2. *Le, la, les* precede the verb, except in the imperative affirmative, e.g.:

Imperative affirmative: Prenez-les, *take them.*
Imperative negative: Ne les prenez pas, *don't take them.*

3. Pronouns which follow the verb are joined to the verb by a hyphen, e.g. *Entrez-vous? Apportez-le!*

4. ce livre, *this* or *that book.*
cet hôtel, *this* or *that hotel.*
cette chaise, *this* or *that chair.*
ces gâteaux, *these* or *those cakes.*

If there is no distinction made between several objects of the same kind, no difference is made between 'this' and 'that', 'these' and 'those'.

Ce is used with masculine nouns.
Cette is used with feminine nouns.
Ces is used with nouns in the plural.
Cet is a special form for use with masculine nouns beginning with a vowel or *h* mute.

If a distinction is made between the nearer and less near, *-ci* is added to the noun for 'this' (or 'these'), and *-là* for 'that' (or 'those').

5. voici, *here is, here are.*
voilà, *there is, there are.*

31

Leçon Cinq

Son père   Sa mère   Son père   Sa mère

Ses parents   Ses parents

Mon cousin   Ma cousine

Leurs enfants

Le bébé   Le garçon   La fillette

LA FAMILLE

A : *Un monsieur.*   B : *Une dame.*

A *(montrant[1] une photographie de ses parents)* : Voici mon père*
et ma mère.*

B *(regardant la photographie)* : Votre père est grand, n'est-ce pas?

A : Oui, il est assez[2] grand.

B : Votre mère n'est pas aussi grande que votre père?

A : Elle est beaucoup[3] plus petite[4] que mon père.

B : Combien de[5] frères et de sœurs avez-vous?

A : Cinq. — Trois frères et deux sœurs. Voici une photographie de
mes parents avec tous[6] leurs enfants.

B : Qui est cette dame?

A : C'est ma sœur aînée.[7]

B : Est-elle mariée?

A : Elle est mariée depuis[8] six ans.[9] — Voici une photographie de
ma sœur et de ses enfants.

B : Où est son mari?[10]

A : Il photographie.

B : Quel âge a votre neveu?[11]

A : Il a cinq ans.

B : Est-ce qu'il va[12] déjà[13] à l'école?[14]

A : Non, il est encore[15] trop[16] jeune.[17]

B : Et quel âge a votre nièce?

A : Elle a onze mois.[18]

B : Alors[19] vous êtes l'oncle de ces charmants enfants?

A : Oui, je suis leur[20] oncle.

[1] *showing.*
[2] *rather.*
[3] *much.*
[4] plus petit(e), *smaller.*
[5] combien (de), *how many.*
[6] *all.*
[7] *elder.*
[8] *since.*
[9] six ans, *six years.*
[10] le mari, *husband.*

[11] le neveu, *nephew.*
[12] il va, *he goes, he is going.*
[13] *already.*
[14] une école, *school.*
[15] *still.*
[16] *too.*
[17] *young.*
[18] le mois, *month.*
[19] *so.*
[20] *their.*

33

1.

Voici	mon père.	*Here is*	*my father.*
Voilà	ma mère.	*There is*	*my mother.*
C'est	mon frère.	*It is*	*my brother.*
Ce n'est pas	ma sœur.	*It is not*	*my sister.*
	mon oncle.		*my uncle.*
	ma tante.		*my aunt.*
	mon cousin.		*my cousin (m.).*
	ma cousine.		*my cousin (f.).*
	mon grand-père.		*my grandfather.*
	ma grand'mère.		*my grandmother.*
	mon beau-père.		*my father-in-law.*
	ma belle-mère.		*my mother-in-law.*
	mon beau-frère.		*my brother-in-law.*
	ma belle-sœur.		*my sister-in-law.*

2.

Voici	mes parents.	*Here are*	*my parents.*
Voilà	mes grands-parents.	*There are*	*my grandparents.*
Ce sont	mes enfants.	*They are*	*my children.*
Ce ne sont pas	mes petits-enfants.	*They are*	*my grandchildren.*
	mes beaux-parents.	*not*	*my parents-in-law.*

3.

Votre	mouchoir	est	bleu.	*Your*	*handkerchief*	*is*	*blue.*
Mon	col		rouge.	*My*	*collar*		*red.*
Son	chapeau		vert.	*His*	*hat*		*green.*
	manteau		gris.	*(or her)*	*coat*		*grey.*
	parapluie		brun.		*umbrella*		*brown.*
	pardessus		blanc.		*overcoat*		*white.*
	gilet		noir.		*waistcoat*		*black.*
			jaune.				*yellow.*

4.

Votre	cravate	est	bleue.	*Your*	*tie*	*is*	*blue.*
Ma	blouse		rouge.	*My*	*blouse*		*red.*
Sa	robe		verte.	*His*	*dress*		*green.*
	chemise		grise.	*(or her)*	*shirt*		*grey.*
			blanche.				*white.*
			brune.				*brown.*
			noire.				*black.*
			jaune.				*yellow.*

5.

Leurs	pantalons	sont	dans l'armoire.
Vos	gants		dans le tiroir.
Nos	bas		sur la coiffeuse.
Mes	chaussettes		sous le fauteuil.
Ses	lunettes		
	pantoufles		

Their	*trousers*	*are*	*in the wardrobe.*
Your	*gloves*		*in the drawer.*
Our	*stockings*		*on the dressing-table.*
My	*socks*		*under the armchair.*
His (or	*glasses*		
her)	*slippers*		

6. Où est mon parapluie?	*Where is my umbrella?*
Est-ce votre parapluie?	*Is this your umbrella?*
Le voici.	*Here it is.*
Le voilà.	*There it is.*
Où est ma canne?	*Where is my walking-stick?*
La voici.	*Here it is.*
La voilà.	*There it is.*
Où sont mes gants?	*Where are my gloves?*
Ils ne sont pas ici.	*They are not here.*
Ne sont-ils pas dans la poche de votre pardessus?	*Aren't they in your overcoat pocket?*
Ah, les voici.	*Oh, here they are.*
Comment est votre pardessus?	*What is your overcoat like?*
Il est noir.	*It is black.*
Comment est son chapeau?	*What is his (or her) hat like?*
Il est vert.	*It is green.*
C'est un petit chapeau vert.	*It is a small green hat.*
Comment sont ses souliers?	*What are his (or her) shoes like?*
Ils sont bruns.	*They are brown.*
Ce sont de grands souliers bruns.	*They are large brown shoes.*

EXPLANATIONS

1. Possessive adjectives:

	Singular		Plural
	MASC.	FEM.[1]	MASC. AND FEM.
my	mon	ma	mes
his, her	son	sa	ses
your (familiar)[2]	ton	ta	tes
your		votre	vos
our		notre	nos
their		leur	leurs

These agree with the noun possessed and not (as in English) with the possessor: e.g. *son chapeau* is the French for both 'his hat' and 'her hat', because *chapeau* is masculine.

2. C'est, *this is, that is, it is.*
   Ce sont, *these are, those are, they are.*
   Écoutez ceci, *listen to this.*
   Regardez cela, *look at that.*

---

[1] *In front of feminine nouns commencing with a vowel,* mon, ton, son *are used instead of* ma, ta, sa; *e.g.,* mon auto, *my car.*
[2] *Used when talking to children, near relatives, close friends.*

In colloquial speech *cela* is often replaced by *ça*:

> Donnez-moi ça, *give me that.*

3. On frappe, *there is a knock at the door; someone is knocking.*
On sonne, *the bell is ringing.*

4. Some adjectives ending in -*c* change -*c* to -*che* to form the feminine, e.g.:

> blanc, blanche, *white*   sec, sèche, *dry.*

Others change -*c* to -*que* (in order to preserve the sound of the final consonant), e.g.:

> public, publique.

For the same reason -*g* changes to -*gue*:

> long, longue.

Adjectives ending in -*f* change to -*ve*:

> neuf, neuve, *new.*

Those ending in -*x* change to -*se*:

> heureux, heureuse, *happy.*

Adjectives ending in -*er* and some ending in -*et* take an *'accent grave'*:

> cher, chère, *dear*   complet, complète.[1]

---

[1] *Also* concret, discret (indiscret), secret, inquiet *(anxious, uneasy); others double the* t: muet, muette *(silent).*

Leçon Six

Du café

Des croissants

Du lait

Du sucre

Du beurre

Une tasse de café

LE PETIT DÉJEUNER

A : *Un monsieur.*   B : *Le garçon.*

(Le garçon frappe à la porte de la chambre du[1] monsieur.)

A : Qui[2] est-ce?

B : C'est moi, le garçon. J'apporte[3] le petit déjeuner.[4]

A : Entrez!

B : Bonjour, monsieur.

A : Bonjour. Qu'est-ce qu'il y a[5] pour le petit déjeuner?

B : Du café,* du lait,* du beurre,* et des croissants.*

A : Mais où est le sucre?* Vous l'avez oublié?[6]

B : Oh, pardon, monsieur. Je l'ai oublié. Je vais[7] le monter[8] tout de suite.[9]

(Le garçon sort,[10] mais revient[11] bientôt[12] avec le sucrier.[13])

[1] of the.	[8] bring up.
[2] who.	[9] tout de suite, *straightaway.*
[3] j'apporte, *I bring.*	[10] il sort, *he goes out.*
[4] le petit déjeuner, *breakfast.*	[11] il revient, *he comes back.*
[5] il y a, *there is, there are.*	[12] soon.
[6] forgotten.	[13] le sucrier, *sugar-bowl.*
[7] je vais, *I am going to.*	

B : Voici le sucre, monsieur. Combien[1] de morceaux prenez-vous?[2]

A : Deux, s'il vous plaît. Merci. Quelle heure[3] est-il?

B : Huit heures et demie.[4]

A : À quelle heure arrive le courrier?[5]

B : Vers[6] huit heures. Je vais demander[7] s'il[8] y a quelque chose[9] pour monsieur.

[1] how much, how many.
[2] le morceau, piece, lump.
[3] quelle heure, what time.
[4] huit heures et demie, half past eight.
[5] mail.
[6] towards.
[7] to ask.
[8] si, if (the i is omitted here in front of the vowel).
[9] quelque chose, something.

FLUENCY PRACTICE

1.

J'ai		du pain.	*I have*		*bread.*	
Je mange		du beurre.	*I eat*		*butter.*	
		du fromage.			*cheese.*	
Il	a	du gâteau.	*He*	*has*	*cake.*	
Elle	mange	du pâté.	*She*	*eats*	*pie.*	
On		de la viande.	*One*		*meat.*	
		de la soupe.			*soup.*	
Ils	ont	de la salade.	*They* (m.)	*have*	*salad.*	
Elles	mangent	des sardines.	*They* (f.)	*eat*	*sardines.*	
		des légumes.			*vegetables.*	
Nous avons		des biscuits.	*We have*		*biscuits.*	
Nous mangeons		des biscottes.	*We eat*		*rusks.*	
		des petits pains.			*rolls.*	
Vous avez		des fruits.	*You have*		*fruit.*	
Vous mangez		des croissants.	*You eat*		*'croissants'.*	

2.

Je n'ai pas		de	pain.	*I have no*			*bread.*
Je ne mange pas			beurre.	*I don't eat*			*butter.*
			fromage.				*cheese.*
Il	n'a pas		viande.	*He*	*has no*		*meat.*
Elle	ne mange pas		salade.	*She*	*doesn't eat*		*salad.*
On			soupe.	*One*			*soup.*
			sardines.				*sardines.*
Ils	n'ont pas		fruits.	*They* (m.)	*have no*		*fruit.*
Elles	ne mangent pas		biscuits.	*They* (f.)	*don't eat*		*biscuits.*

3.

N'ai-je pas	de sucre?	*Have I*	*no*	*sugar?*
N'a-t-il pas	de café?	*Has he*		*coffee?*
N'a-t-elle pas	de crème?	*Has she*		*cream?*
N'ont-ils pas	de lait?	*Have they* (m.)		*milk?*
N'ont-elles pas	de vin?	*Have they* (f.)		*wine?*
N'avons-nous pas	de bière?	*Have we*		*beer?*
N'avez-vous pas	d'oranges?	*Have you*		*oranges?*

4. Je l'ai.   *I have it.*
Je les ai.   *I have them.*
J'en ai.   *I have some.*
Je ne l'ai pas.   *I haven't got it.*
Je ne les ai pas.   *I haven't got them.*
Je n'en ai pas.   *I haven't any.*

5. Vous l'avez.   *You have it.*
Vous les avez.   *You have them.*
Vous en avez.   *You have some.*
Ne l'avez-vous pas?   *Haven't you got it?*
Ne les avez-vous pas?   *Haven't you got them?*
N'en avez-vous pas?   *Haven't you any?*

6. Nous l'avons.   *We have it.*
Nous les avons.   *We have them.*
Nous en avons.   *We have some.*
Nous ne l'avons pas.   *We haven't got it.*
Nous ne les avons pas.   *We haven't got them.*
Nous n'en avons pas.   *We haven't any.*

7. Il (elle) l'a.   *He (she) has it.*
Il (elle) les a.   *He (she) has them.*
Il (elle) en a.   *He (she) has some.*
L'a-t-il (-elle)?   *Has he (she) got it?*
Les a-t-il (-elle)?   *Has he (she) got them?*
En a-t-il (-elle)?   *Has he (she) got some?*

Ils (elles) l'ont.   *They have it.*
Ils (elles) les ont.   *They have them.*
Ils (elles) en ont.   *They have some.*
L'ont-ils (elles)?   *Have they got it?*
Les ont-ils (-elles)?   *Have they got them?*
En ont-ils (-elles)?   *Have they any?*

9. QUELLE HEURE EST-IL?   WHAT TIME IS IT?
Il est une heure.   *It is one o'clock.*
Il est deux heures.   *It is two o'clock.*
Il est trois heures.   *It is three o'clock.*
Il est quatre heures.   *It is four o'clock.*
Il est cinq heures.   *It is five o'clock.*
Il est six heures.   *It is six o'clock.*
Il est sept heures.   *It is seven o'clock.*
Il est huit heures.   *It is eight o'clock.*
Il est neuf heures.   *It is nine o'clock.*
Il est dix heures.   *It is ten o'clock.*
Il est onze heures.   *It is eleven o'clock.*
Il est midi.   *It is twelve noon.*
Il est minuit.   *It is midnight.*

1. *du* = 'some' (*or* 'any'), in front of a masculine noun in the singular.
   de la = 'some' (*or* 'any'), in front of a feminine noun in the singular.
   de l' = 'some' (*or* 'any'), in front of a noun in the singular commencing with a vowel or *h* mute.
   des = 'some' (*or* 'any'), in front of a noun in the plural.

2. Distinguish between the following:

   The definite article: *le, la, les.*
   The indefinite article: *un, une.*
   The partitive article: *du, de la, des.*

Each noun must be preceded by one of these articles.

Where in English no article at all is used, as in 'We have meat for dinner,' 'Does he sell matches?' etc., French uses the partitive article, e.g.:

   Nous avons de la viande pour le dîner. Est-ce qu'il vend des allumettes? etc.

3. In the negative, *de* replaces *du, de la,* or *des,* e.g.:
   Je n'ai pas d'argent, *I have no money.*

4. *En* (some, any, of it, of them) replaces any noun used with the partitive article, e.g.:
   Avez-vous des cigarettes? Je n'en ai pas.

5. Nouns and adjectives ending in *-al* change this ending to *-aux* in the plural, e.g.:

le cheval, *horse*	les chevaux
principal, *principal*	principaux

Nouns and adjectives ending in *-eau* or *-eu* add *-x* in plural:

	le chapeau, *hat*	les chapeaux
	beau, *beautiful*	beaux
	le cheveu, *hair*	les cheveux
Exceptions:	bleu, *blue*	bleus
	le pneu, *tyre*	les pneus

40

Leçon Sept

de la bière

de l'eau

du vin

un verre de bière

une carafe d'eau

une bouteille de vin

LE CAFÉ

A : *Un monsieur.*   B : *Un autre monsieur.*   C : *Le garçon de café.*

A : Bonjour, Monsieur Boulin, comment allez-vous?[1]

B : Très bien, merci, et vous?

A : Pas trop[2] bien.

B : Qu[3]'avez-vous?

A : J'ai un lumbago. Comment va Madame Boulin?

B : Ma femme va très bien, je vous remercie.[4]

---

[1] comment allez-vous? *how are you?*
[2] *too.*
[3] que, *what.*
[4] *thank.*

A : Et les enfants? Ils vont[F] bien?

B : Tout le monde[1] est en bonne santé,[2] Dieu merci.

A : Voulez-vous prendre[3] un verre* avec moi?

B : Avec plaisir.

A : Il y a un café en face.[4] Passons de l'autre[5] côté[6] de la rue.

(Ils traversent la rue et trouvent[7] deux places à la terrasse d'un café.)

C : Vous désirez, messieurs?

A : Que prenez[F] -vous?

B : Un verre de bière.*

A : Moi, je n'aime pas la bière. Je prends[F] une tasse de café.

C : Nature[8] ou crème?

A : Au lait,[9] s'il vous plaît.

(Le garçon entre dans le café et revient bientôt avec le verre de bière et la tasse de café.)

A : L'addition,[10] s'il vous plaît.

C : Soixante-dix[11] la bière et cinquante-cinq[12] le café. Un franc et vingt-cinq[13] centimes, monsieur.

A : Je n'ai pas de monnaie.[14] Pouvez-vous me changer un billet[15] de dix[16] francs?

C : Certainement, monsieur — soixante-quinze[17] centimes et huit francs qui[18] font[19] dix.

A (*lui[20] donnant[21] vingt centimes*) : Voilà pour vous.

C : Merci, monsieur.

[1] tout le monde, *everybody.*
[2] la santé, *health.*
[3] *to take.*
[4] en face, *opposite.*
[5] *other.*
[6] le côté, *side.*
[7] *find.*
[8] café nature = café noir.
[9] le lait, *milk.*
[10] l'addition (*f.*), *bill*
[11] *seventy.*
[12] *fifty-five.*
[13] *twenty-five.*
[14] la monnaie, *small change.*
[15] le billet, *note.*
[16] *ten.*
[17] *seventy-five.*
[18] *which.*
[19] *make.*
[20] lui, (*to*) *him.*
[21] *giving.*

FLUENCY PRACTICE

1.

Les messieurs	entrent.	The gentlemen	are	going[1] in.
Les dames	rentrent.	The ladies		going[1] back.
Les garçons	montent.	The boys		going[1] up.
Les fillettes	travaillent.	The girls		working.
Les professeurs	jouent.	The teachers		playing.
Les élèves		The pupils		

2.

*Est-ce que ce sont	les musiciens	Are they	the musicians
Est-ce que ce ne sont pas	les acteurs	Aren't they	the actors
	les danseurs		the dancers
Oui, ce sont	les facteurs	Yes, they are	the postmen
Non, ce ne sont pas	les pompiers	No, they aren't	the firemen

* *Note that this table contains both statements and questions. Punctuation has therefore been omitted.*

3.

Est-ce que	les garçons	entrent?	Are	the boys	going[1] in?
	les acteurs	montent?		the actors	going[1] up?
	les pompiers	rentrent?		the firemen	going[1] back?

Oui, ils	entrent.	Yes, they are	(going[1] in).
	montent.		(going[1] up).
	rentrent.		(going[1] back).

Non, ils	ne montent pas.	No, they are not	(going[1] up).
	ne rentrent pas.		(going[1] back).
	n'entrent pas.		(going[1] in).

4.

Est-ce que	les fillettes	dansent?	Are	the girls	dancing?
	les actrices	chantent?		the actresses	singing?
	les danseuses	jouent?		the dancers	playing?

Oui, elles	dansent.	Yes, they are	(dancing).
	chantent.		(singing).
	jouent.		(playing).

Non, elles ne	dansent	pas.	No, they are not	(dancing).
	chantent			(singing).
	jouent			(playing).

5.

Je viens		du théâtre.	I come[2]			from the	theatre.
Il	vient	du cinéma.	He	comes			cinema.
Elle		du café.	She				café.
Ils	viennent	de la gare.	They (m.)		come		station.
Elles		de la poste.	(f.)				post-office.
Nous venons		de la bibliothèque.	We come				library.
Vous venez		de l'école.	You come				school.
		de l'église.					church.

[1] or *coming*.   [2] or *am coming, etc.*

43

6.

C'est le chapeau	de Jean.	It is	John's	hat.
	de Marie.		Mary's	
	du professeur.		the teacher's	
	du curé.		the priest's	
	de la petite fille.		the little girl's	
	de l'élève.		the pupil's	
	de l'étudiant.		the student's	

Ce sont les gants	des professeurs.	They are	the teachers'	gloves.
	des enfants.		the children's	
	de Jean et de Marie.		John's and Mary's	

7.

Je vais		au théâtre.	I am		going to the	theatre.
Il	va	au cinéma.	He	is		cinema.
Elle		au café.	She			café.
		à la gare.				station.
Ils	vont	à la poste.	They (m.)	are		post-office.
Elles		à la pharmacie.	They (f.)			chemist's.
		à l'église.				church.
Nous allons		à l'école.	We	are		school.
Vous allez			You			

8.

Je prends		du thé.	I take		tea.
Il	prend	de la bière.	He	takes	beer
Elle		un jus de fruits.	She		a fruit juice.
		un grand verre de vin rouge.			a large glass of red wine.
Ils	prennent	un petit verre de vin blanc.	They (m.)	take	a small glass of white wine.
Elles		une grande bouteille de bière blonde.	They (f.)		a large bottle of light beer.
Nous prenons		une petite bouteille de bière brune.	We		a small bottle of dark beer.
Vous prenez		une tasse de café au lait.	You		a cup of milk coffee.

9.

Prenez-	le	à midi cinq.	Take	it (m.)	at five past twelve
Apportez-	la		Bring	it (f.)	(noon).
Mangez-	les	à une heure et quart.	Eat	them	at quarter past one.
Buvez-	en	à deux heures et demie.	Drink	some	at half past two.
		à trois heures moins le quart.			at quarter to three.
		à cinq heures moins dix.			at ten to five.
		le matin.			in the morning.
		l'après-midi.			in the afternoon.
		le soir.			in the evening.

44

EXPLANATIONS

1. The infinitive of most verbs ends in *-er* (pronounced like *é*), e.g. *marcher*, to walk, *donner*, to give, *trouver*, to find, etc.

Verbs in *-er* follow a regular pattern:

> In connection with *je, il, elle* or *on* they end in *-e*.
> In connection with *ils* or *elles* they end in *-ent*.
> In connection with *nous* they end in *-ons*.
> In connection with *vous* they end in *-ez*.
> In connection with *tu*[1] they end in *-es*.

Note   (*a*) These endings are added to the stem of the verb, i.e., *march-, donn-, trouv-*, etc.

            (*b*) The endings *-e, -es* and *-ent* are silent.

2. Verbs which do not follow a regular pattern are called irregular verbs. Some of the most important irregular verbs are: *aller*, to go; *venir*, to come; *prendre*, to take (see Fluency Practice).

Another important irregular verb, of which examples will be found on pages 29 and 30, is *mettre*, to put *(je mets, il met, nous mettons, vous mettez, ils mettent)*.

3. *du* is used instead of *de le*.
  des replaces *de les*.

Note. There are no corresponding contractions for *de la* or *de l'*.

4. *au* is used for *à le*.
  aux instead of *à les*.

Note   (*a*) Both *au* and *aux* are pronounced alike, except in liaison. (See page 97, 1).

            (*b*) There are no corresponding contractions for *à la* or *à l'*.

5. There is no equivalent in French to the English possessive case in *'s*. 'The baker's wife' is 'the wife of the baker' (*la femme du boulanger*). 'Anne's pretty frock' is 'the pretty frock of Anne' (*la jolie robe d'Anne*), etc.

---

[1] *Used when speaking to children, near relations, close friends.*

Leçon Huit

Le poisson (un hareng)

Le fromage
(Une assiette de fromages)

Les fruits
(Une corbeille de fruits)

Le potage
(crème de chou-fleur)

Les légumes
(Un plat de légumes)

La viande
(rôti de veau)

LE REPAS

AU RESTAURANT

A : *Un monsieur.*   B : *Une demoiselle.*   C : *Le garçon.*

C : Voici le menu.

A : Est-ce que vous prenez du potage,* mademoiselle?

B : Non, je n'aime pas le potage pour le déjeuner.

A : Ni moi non plus.[1] Qu'est-ce qu'il y a comme hors-d'œuvre?

C : Des sardines, des filets de hareng,* du saucisson,[2] du pâté[3] de foie,[4] des radis,[5] des olives, des betteraves.[6]

B : Je prendrai[E] du pâté de foie.

A : Une salade de betteraves pour moi.

C : Et ensuite[7] du poisson,* de la viande?*

[1] ni moi non plus, *neither do I.*
[2] le saucisson, *(dry) sausage.*
[3] le pâté, *paste.*
[4] le foie, *liver.*
[5] le radis, *radish.*
[6] la betterave, *beetroot.*
[7] *afterwards.*

46

A : Apportez d'abord[1] les hors-d'œuvre. Laissez[2]-nous la carte du jour.

C : Bien, monsieur.

A : Mangerez-vous du poisson? Il y a du saumon,[3] de la truite,[4] des soles frites.[5]

B : Non, je ne prendrai pas de poisson. Quelles viandes y a-t-il?

A : Du veau, du rosbif,[6] des côtes[7] de porc. Il y a aussi du gibier[8] et de la volaille.[9]

B : Qu'est-ce que vous prenez?

A : Du veau aux petits pois.[10] C'est la spécialité de la maison.

B : Alors je prendrai la même chose.[11]

A : Et comme salade? De la laitue?[12]

B : D'accord.[13]

[1] first.
[2] laisser, to leave, to let have.
[3] le saumon, salmon.
[4] la truite, trout.
[5] fried.
[6] le rosbif, roast beef.
[7] la côte, rib.

[8] le gibier, game.
[9] la volaille, poultry.
[10] les petits pois, peas.
[11] la même chose, the same thing.
[12] la laitue, lettuce.
[13] d'accord, short for je suis d'accord, I agree.

FLUENCY PRACTICE

1.

Je bois	du thé.	I drink	tea.
Tu bois	du café.	You drink	coffee.
Il boit	du cacao.	He drinks	cocoa.
Elle boit	de la bière.	She drinks	beer.
Ils boivent	de la limonade.	They drink	lemonade.
Elles boivent	du jus de fruits.		fruit juice.
Nous buvons	du jus d'oranges.	We drink	orange juice.
Vous buvez	du jus de tomates.	You drink	tomato juice.

2.

J'ai		faim.	I am		hungry.
Tu as		soif.	You are		thirsty.
Il	a	chaud.	He	is	hot.
Elle		froid.	She		cold.
		raison.			right.
Ils	ont	tort.	They are		wrong.
Elles		peur.			afraid.
Nous avons		sommeil.	We	are	sleepy.
Vous avez			You		

47

3.

Je mange	beaucoup	de	viande.
Je ne mange pas	peu		poisson.
Tu manges	trop		légumes.
Tu ne manges pas	assez		fruits.
Vous mangez			salade.
Vous ne mangez pas			soupe.
Nous mangeons			
Nous ne mangeons pas			

I eat	much		meat.
I don't eat	little		fish.
You eat	too much (many)		vegetables.
You don't eat	enough		fruit.
			salad.
We eat			soup.
We don't eat			

4.

Au petit déjeuner	je prends	un œuf à la coque.
Au déjeuner	tu prends	des œufs brouillés.
Au dîner	il prend	des œufs sur le plat.
Comme hors-d'œuvre	elle prend	une omelette aux champignons.
Ensuite	ils prennent	du pâté de foie.
Comme dessert	elles prennent	de la glace aux fraises.
	nous prenons	du potage à l'oseille.
	vous prenez	

For breakfast	I take	a boiled egg.
For lunch	you take	scrambled eggs.
For dinner	he takes	fried eggs.
As hors-d'œuvre	she takes	a mushroom omelette.
After that	they take	liver paste.
As dessert		strawberry ice.
	we take	sorrel soup.
	you take	

5.

Le	canif	est	en	or.
Ce	parapluie			plastique.
Mon	mouchoir			toile.
Son	chapeau			paille.
				fer.
La	clef			soie.
Cette	cravate			argent.
Ma	montre			coton.
Sa	robe			feutre.
				cuir.
Les	souliers	sont		laine.
Ces	gants			nylon.
Mes	chaussettes			papier.
Ses	bas			nickel.
Nos	couteaux			
Vos	fourchettes			
Leurs	cuillères			

The	penknife	is	of¹	gold.
This	umbrella			plastic.
My	handkerchief			linen.
His (her)	hat			straw.
				iron.
The	key			silk.
This	tie			silver.
My	watch			cotton.
His (her)	dress			felt.
				leather.
The	shoes	are		wool.
These	gloves			nylon.
My	socks			paper.
His (her)	stockings			nickel.
Our	knives			
Your	forks			
Their	spoons			

¹ i.e. 'made of'.

6.

Je mangerai Je prendrai J'aurai			I shall		
Tu	mangeras prendras auras		You will		
Il Elle	mangera prendra aura		He She } will		
Ils Elles	mangeront prendront auront		They will		
Nous	mangerons prendrons aurons		We shall		
Vous	mangerez prendrez aurez		You will		

du poisson.	eat	fish.
du rôti.	take	joint.
du potage.	have	soup.
de la viande.		meat.
de la compote.		salad.
des légumes.		stewed fruit.
des fruits.		vegetables.
des petits pois.		fruit.
des haricots verts.		peas.
des épinards.		French beans.
		spinach.

7.

Je serai J'irai		I shall	
Tu	seras iras	You will	
Il Elle	sera ira	He She } will	
Ils Elles	seront iront	They will	
Nous	serons irons	We shall	
Vous	serez irez	You will	

à Paris	be in	Paris	to-night.
en France	go to	France	to-morrow.
en Angleterre		England	the day after to-morrow.
en Écosse		Scotland	next Monday.
en Belgique		Belgium	next week.
en Suisse		Switzerland	to-day week.
au Danemark		Denmark	to-day fortnight.
au Maroc		Morocco	in three weeks.
au Portugal		Portugal	from Tuesday onwards.
aux États-Unis		the United States	

ce soir.
demain.
après-demain.
lundi prochain.
la semaine prochaine.
d'aujourd'hui en huit.
d'aujourd'hui en quinze.
dans trois semaines.
à partir de mardi.

49

EXPLANATIONS

1. The future tense of verbs is formed by adding certain endings to the infinitive. These endings are the same as those of the present tense of *avoir* (see Lesson VI). Verbs ending in *-re* drop the *-e* before the ending of the future, e.g., *prendre*, to take; *je prendrai*, I shall take.

The future of *aller*, to go, is *j'irai, tu iras, il ira*, etc.

The future of *venir*, to come, is *je viendrai, tu viendras*, etc.

The future of *être*, to be, is *je serai, tu seras*, etc.

The future of *avoir*, to have, is *j'aurai, tu auras*, etc.

2. Adverbs denoting a quantity like *beaucoup*, much, *peu*, little, *trop*, too much, *combien*, how much, *assez*, enough, *plus*, more, *moins*, less, etc., are followed before a noun by *de*.

Exceptions: bien des livres, *lots of books*.
　　　　　　　encore du vin, *some more wine*.
　　　　　　　la plupart des gens, *most people*.

3. J'ai faim, *I am hungry (lit. I have hunger)*.

Note that 'to be hungry, thirsty, sleepy, afraid, cold, hot' are expressed by 'to have hunger, thirst', etc.

4. In the present tense, the familiar form of verbs which do not follow the *-er* pattern (see page 45(1)) is identical with the form of the verb used with *je*, e.g. *je prends, tu prends: je bois, tu bois : je viens, tu viens*. Exceptions are *je vais, tu vas : j'ai, tu as : je suis, tu es*.

The imperative in the familiar form is the same as the form of the verb used with *tu* in the present tense, except that verbs in *-er* drop the final *-s*, e.g. *mange*, eat! *va*, go!* *viens*, come!

*but note *vas-y*.

Leçon Neuf

une bicyclette   un scooter   une moto(cyclette)*
un vélo*

une auto(mobile)*   un (auto)bus*   un (auto)car*

* The shorter forms are used in conversation.

À L'Arrêt[1] d'Autobus

A : 1er *monsieur.*   B : 2ème *monsieur.*   C : 3ème *monsieur.*

D : *le receveur du premier autobus.*   E : *le receveur du deuxième autobus.*

A : L'Avenue Mozart, est-ce loin[2] d'ici?[F]

B : À peu près[3] quarante minutes de marche.[4] Vous pouvez[F] prendre ou[5] le métro ou[5] l'autobus.

A : Je préfère l'autobus.

B : Il y a un arrêt d'autobus tout près[6] d'ici. Vous tournez à gauche et montez la rue jusqu'au[7] passage clouté.[8] Vous traversez et continuez jusqu'à la deuxième rue à droite.

---

[1] un arrêt, *stop.*
[2] *far.*
[3] à peu près, *approximately.*
[4] de marche, *on foot.*
[5] ou . . . ou, *either . . or.*
[6] tout près, *quite near.*
[7] jusqu'à, *until, as far as.*
[8] clouté, *studded (i.e. pedestrian crossing).*

Prenez cette rue et vous verrez[1] l'arrêt d'autobus à votre gauche.

A : Quel autobus dois-je[2] prendre?

B : Le 42 vous y[3] conduira[4] directement.

. . . . .

A : Est-ce bien l'arrêt pour aller à l'Avenue Mozart?

C : C'est bien ici. Prenez le 42. (*Prenant*[5] *un numero d'ordre*[6] *d'un distributeur*[7] *automatique)* Voici votre numéro.

A : Je dois avoir[8] un numéro pour monter dans l'autobus?

C : Mais oui, monsieur. Comme vous voyez, il y a beaucoup de gens[9] qui attendent[10] l'autobus. Alors[11] chaque personne prend un numéro. Quand[12] l'autobus arrive on monte dans l'ordre des numéros. Ainsi vous montez avant[13] les personnes qui arrivent après[14] vous.

A : C'est une bonne idée.

C : Voilà l'autobus qui[15] arrive.

D : Les numéros s'il vous plaît. Montez le premier.[F]   *(Une dame lui*[16] *montre son numéro.)*

D : Soixante-neuf,[17]
    soixante-dix,
    soixante et onze,
    soixante-douze,
    soixante-treize,
    soixante-quatorze,
    soixante-quinze,
    soixante-seize,
    soixante-dix-sept.
    Complet.[18] Il n'y a plus[19] de place.

C : Voilà un autre autobus. Il y a assez de place.

[1] vous verrez, *you will see.*
[2] je dois, *I must.*
[3] *there.*
[4] *will take.*
[5] *taking.*
[6] *serial number.*
[7] *machine.*
[8] *have.*
[9] les gens *(f. pl.), people.*
[10] attendre, *to wait for.*
[11] *so.*
[12] *when.*
[13] *before.*
[14] *after.*
[15] *who, which.*
[16] *to him, to her.*
[17] *see page 15.*
[18] *full up.*
[19] ne . . . plus, *no more.*

E : Soixante-dix-huit,
   soixante-dix-neuf,
   quatre vingts,
   quatre-vingt-un,
   quatre-vingt-deux,
   quatre-vingt-trois.

C : C'est votre tour.[1]

A : Merci beaucoup. *(Il monte dans l'autobus.)*

[1] le tour, *turn.*

FLUENCY PRACTICE

1. C'est | un beau parc. | It is | *a beautiful park.*
   | un bel enfant. | | *a beautiful child.*
   | une belle robe. | | *a beautiful dress.*
   | un joli porte-monnaie. | | *a pretty purse.*
   | une bonne idée. | | *a good idea.*
   | un bon hôtel. | | *a good hotel.*
   | un vieux château. | | *an old castle.*
   | une vieille église. | | *an old church.*
   | une jeune femme. | | *a young woman.*
   | un nouveau professeur. | | *a new teacher.*
   | une nouvelle chanson. | | *a new song.*
   | un livre intéressant. | | *an interesting book.*
   | une femme intelligente. | | *an intelligent woman.*
   | un petit dictionnaire anglais. | | *a little English dictionary.*
   | une bonne petite voiture. | | *a good little car.*

2. Ce sont | de bons camarades. | They are | *good friends.*
   | de nouveaux élèves. | | *new pupils.*
   | de mauvaises habitudes. | | *bad habits.*
   | des journaux français. | | *French newspapers.*
   | des livres amusants. | | *funny books.*
   | des petits chats noirs. | | *black kittens.*

3.

Le premier	chapeau	bleu.	The first	blue	hat.
Le dernier	pardessus	noir.	The last	black	overcoat.
Le même	costume	blanc.	The same	white	costume.
Le seul	veston	rouge.	The only	red	coat.
L'autre	gilet	brun.	The other	brown	waistcoat.
Le grand	pantalon	vert.	The big	green	trousers.
Le petit	complet	gris.	The small	grey	suit.
Un bon			A good		
Un meilleur			A better		
Un autre[1]			Another[1]		
Encore un[2]			Another[2]		
Le meilleur			The best		

[1] *i.e. a different one.*   [2] *i.e., an additional one.*

53

4.

La première	robe	bleue.	The first	blue	dress.
La dernière	blouse	noire.	The last	black	blouse.
La même	cravate	blanche.	The same	white	tie.
La seule	jupe	rouge.	The only	red	skirt.
L'autre	jacquette	brune.	The other	brown	jacket.
La grande	manchette	verte.	The big	green	cuff.
La petite	chaussette	grise.	The small	grey	sock.
Une bonne			A good		
Une meilleure			A better		
Une autre[1]			Another[1]		
Encore une[2]			Another[2]		

[1] i.e., a different one.   [2] i.e., an additional one.

5.

Il est	très	facile.	It[E] is	very	easy.
Elle	si	difficile.		so	difficult.
	bien	long(ue).		rather	long.
C'est	trop	court(e).	This	too	short.
	assez	gros(se).	That	fairly	thick.
	un peu	mince.	It[E]	a little	thin.
	beaucoup trop	large		far too	wide.
		étroit(e).			narrow.

6.

J'ai déjà	du pain	mais je n'ai pas	de beurre.
	de la viande		de sel.
	des cigarettes		d'allumettes.
	du beurre		de confitures.
	de la bière		de verre.
	du jambon		d'assiette.

I already have some	bread	but I haven't any	butter.
	meat		salt.
	cigarettes		matches.
	butter		jam.
	beer		glass.
	ham		plate.

J'en ai déjà.   I already have some.

7.

Je	peux	monter.	I	can	get in (or up).
Tu	veux	descendre.	You	wish to	get off (or down).
	dois	continuer.		have to	go on.
		prendre le métro.			take the Underground.
Il	peut	y aller.	He	can	go there.
Elle	veut	traverser la rue.	She	wishes to	cross the road.
	doit	le faire.		has to	do it.
		en profiter.			take advantage of it.
Ils	peuvent		They	can	
Elles	veulent			wish to	
	doivent			have to	
Vous	pouvez		You	can	
	voulez			wish to	
	devez			have to	
Nous	pouvons		We	can	
	voulons			wish to	
	devons			have to	

54

8. Il y a

Il y a					
	du papier	sur la table.	*There is*	*paper*	*on the table.*
	de la ficelle	dans le tiroir.		*string*	*in the drawer.*
	des enveloppes	sous le journal.	*There are*	*envelopes*	*under the newspaper.*

Il n'y en a pas.   *There isn't (aren't) any.*

9. Est-ce

Est-ce				
près	d'ici?	*Is it*	*near*	*here?*
loin	de là?		*far from*	*there?*
	du café?			*the café?*
	de l'hôtel?			*the hotel?*
	de la gare?			*the station?*

10.

Quel autobus	dois-je	prendre?	*Which bus*	*must I*	*take?*
Quelle rue	devons-nous		*Which street*	*must we*	

Quels cigares	préférez-vous?	*Which cigars*	*do you prefer?*
Quelles cigarettes		*Which cigarettes*	

EXPLANATIONS

1. Adjectives usually follow the noun, but some, like *bon, mauvais, grand, petit, joli, beau,* and a few others, precede it.

Adjectives denoting colour or nationality always follow the noun.

2. *il y a* means both 'there is' and 'there are'.

3. *Quel(s)* = 'which', when followed by a masculine noun or nouns.

   Quelle(s) = 'which', when followed by a feminine noun or nouns.

4. The feminine of *beau (bel),* 'beautiful', is *belle.*

The feminine of *nouveau (nouvel),* 'new', is *nouvelle.*

The feminine of *vieux (vieil),* 'old', is *vieille.*

Bel, nouvel and *vieil* are special forms for the masculine when they precede a vowel or *h* mute. They are pronounced the same as the corresponding feminines.

5. *Des* is reduced to *de* before an adjective preceding the noun.

6. It is = *il (elle) est,* according to the gender of the noun previously mentioned.

It is = *c'est,* if the word 'it' does not stand for a noun, but has the same meaning as 'this' or 'that'. If an adjective after *c'est* is used without a noun, it remains invariable, i.e. in its masculine form.

It is = *il est,* when speaking of time (see page 39,9).

Leçon Dix

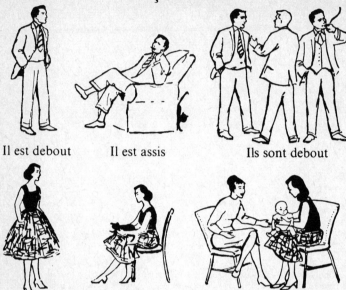

Il est debout   Il est assis   Ils sont debout

Elle est debout   Elle est assise   Elles sont assises

Dans L'Autobus

A : *Un monsieur.*   B : *Un autre monsieur.*   C : *Le receveur.*

C : Les tickets, s'il vous plaît.

A : Avenue Mozart, s'il vous plaît.

C : Deux sections.[1]

A : C'est combien ?

C : Ne voulez-vous pas prendre un carnet ?[2] Cela vous coûtera[3] moins[4] cher.[5] Chaque[6] carnet contient dix tickets.

---

[1] *The bus route is divided into sections. You pay a standard rate for one or two sections.*

[2] *If you buy a folder of ten tickets (called* un carnet*) you get them cheaper. They are also valid on the* métro.

[3] coûter, *to cost.*

[4] *less.*

[5] cher, chère, *dear.*

[6] *each.*

A : Je prendrai donc un carnet. C'est combien?

C : Huit francs, monsieur.

(Monsieur A paie et le receveur lui donne un carnet en retirant[1] deux tickets.)

A *(à un monsieur):* Pardon, monsieur, pourriez-vous[2] me dire[3] quel est ce bel édifice[4] de style grec?[5]

B : C'est l'église[6] de la Madeleine. À droite vous voyez la Rue Royale, une des plus élégantes de Paris. Au bout[7] de cette rue vous voyez la Place de la Concorde.

A : Oui, je l'ai vue[8] hier.[9] Quelle[E] belle place!

[1] retirer, *to take out.*
[2] pourriez-vous? *could you?*
[3] dire, *to say, to tell.*
[4] un édifice, *building.*
[5] grec, grecque, *Greek.*

[6] une église, *church.*
[7] le bout, *end.*
[8] *seen* (j'ai vu, *I saw.*)
[9] *yesterday.*

FLUENCY PRACTICE

1.						
Parlez	au gérant.		*Speak to*	*the manager.*		
Répondez	à la préposée.		*Reply to*	*the woman in charge.*		
Demandez	aux messieurs.		*Ask*	*the gentlemen.*		
Dites	aux dames.		*Tell*	*the ladies.*		
Écrivez	-lui.		*Write to*	*him* (or *her*).		
	-leur			*them.*		
	-moi.			*me.*		
	-nous.			*us.*		

2. Ne	me	parlez	pas.	*Don't*	*speak to*	*me.*
	nous	répondez			*reply to*	*us.*
	lui	demandez			*ask*	*him* (or *her*).
	leur	dites			*tell*	*them.*

3. Je	lui	parle.		*I*	*speak to*	*him* (or *her*).
	leur	réponds.			*reply to*	*them.*
	vous	demande.			*ask*	*you.*
		dis.			*tell*	
		écris.			*write to*	

4. Il	me	parle.		*He*	*speaks to*	*me.*
Elle	nous	répond		*She*	*replies to*	*us.*
	vous	demande.			*asks*	*you.*
	lui	dit.			*tells*	*him* (or *her*).
	leur					*them.*

5.

Ils	me	parlent.		They	speak to	me.
Elles	nous	répondent.			reply	us.
	vous	demandent.			ask	you.
	lui	disent.			tell	him (or her).
	leur					them.

6.

Parlons	au monsieur.		Let us	speak to	the gentleman.
Répondons	à la dame.			reply to	the lady.
Demandons	-lui.			ask	him (or her).
Disons	-leur.			tell	them.
Écrivons				write to	

Ne parlons	pas	à cet homme.		Don't let us	speak	to this man.
N'écrivons		à cette femme.			write	to this woman.
Ne	lui	parlons	pas.			to him (or her).
	leur	écrivons				to them.

7.

Je vais	le faire.		I am going to	do it.
Je veux	l'envoyer		I want to	send it.
Je sais	lui	parler.	I know how to	speak	to	him (or her).
Je peux	leur	écrire.	I can	write		them.
Je dois		répondre.	I have to	reply	

Allez-vous	le faire?		Are you going to	do it?
Voulez-vous	etc.		Do you want to	etc.
Savez-vous			Do you know how to	
Pouvez-vous			Can you	

8.

Je ne sais pas	où.		I don't know	where.
	qui.			who.
	quand.			when.
	comment.			how.
	combien.			how much (how many).
	lequel.			which (replacing a m. noun).
	laquelle.			which (replacing a f. noun).
	lesquels.			which (m. pl.).
	lesquelles.			which (f. pl.).
	quoi.			what.
	pourquoi.			why.

9.

Quel beau tableau!	What a fine painting!
Regardez-le.	Look at it.
Vous l'achetez, n'est-ce pas?	You are buying it, aren't you?
Est-ce qu'il le vend?	Is he selling it?
Je le prendrai s'il le vend.	I'll take it if he sells it.
Quelle belle gravure!	What a fine print!
Regardez-la.	Look at it.
Vous l'achetez, n'est-ce pas?	You are buying it, aren't you?
Est-ce qu'il la vend?	Is he selling it?
Je la prendrai s'il la vend.	I'll take it if he sells it.

Quelles belles images!		What fine pictures!
Regardez-les.		Look at them.
Vous les achetez, n'est-ce pas?		You are buying them, aren't you?
Est-ce qu'il les vend?		Is he selling them?
Je les achèterai s'il les vend.		I'll buy them if he sells them.
Elles ne sont pas à vendre.		They are not for sale.
Quel dommage!		What a pity!

10.	J'attends		l'autobus.	*I*	wait for	the bus.
	J'attendrai		le train.		shall wait for	the train.
	Tu	attends	le tramway.	*You*	wait for	the tram.
		attendras	le métro.		will wait for	the Underground.
	Il	attend	mes amis.	*He*	waits for	my friends.
	Elle	attendra	quelques minutes.	*She*	will wait for	a few minutes.
			quelqu'un.			somebody.
	Ils	attendent		*They*	wait for	
	Elles	attendront			will wait for	
	Nous	attendons		*We*	wait for	
		attendrons			shall wait for	
	Vous	attendez		*You*	wait for	
		attendrez			will wait for	

EXPLANATIONS

1. *Lui* (to him, to her) and *leur* (to them) are indirect object pronouns and must be distinguished from the direct object pronouns *le, la, les* (see Lesson IV); e.g., in the sentence *je le vois*, 'I see him', the word 'him' is the direct object, whereas in *donnez-lui l'argent*, 'give him the money', 'him' is the indirect object, as what you actually give (i.e. the direct object) is 'the money'.

2. *Quel* = 'what a', when followed by a masculine singular noun.
Quelle = 'what a', when followed by a feminine singular noun.
In the plural *-s* is added to both. There is no difference in pronunciation between *quel, quelle, quels* and *quelles*.

3. *Lequel* = 'which', when replacing a masculine singular noun.
Laquelle = 'which', when replacing a feminine singular noun.
Lesquels = 'which', when replacing a masculine plural noun.
Lesquelles = 'which', when replacing a feminine plural noun.

4. The regular pattern of verbs in *-re* is as shown for *attendre*. *Vendre*, to sell, *répondre*, to reply, *descendre*, to go (or come) down, follow the same pattern.

Leçon Onze

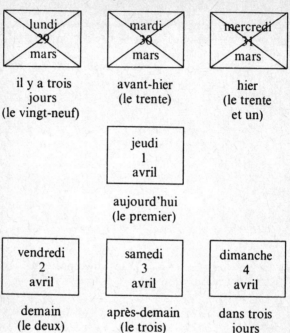

UNE VISITE

A : *Le professeur Lebrun.* B : *Mme. Lebrun.* C : *Leur fille Simone.*
     D : *Charles Walton, un jeune Américain.*

*(Dans l'appartement[1] des Lebrun. Monsieur Lebrun lit[2] son journal.
Mme. Lebrun tricote.[3] Simone écrit[4] une lettre. On sonne.[5])*

B *(à sa fille)*: Veux-tu aller voir ce que[6] c'est?

(Simone va à la porte d'entrée et l'ouvre. C'est Charles qui a sonné.)

D : Est-ce bien ici qu'habite[7] Monsieur Lebrun?

[1] un appartement, *flat.*
[2] lire, *to read.*
[3] tricoter, *to knit.*
[4] écrire, *to write.*

[5] sonner, *to ring.*
[6] ce que, *what.*
[7] habiter, *to dwell, to live.*

C : Oui, c'est ici.

D : Pourrais-je[1] le voir? Je lui apporte la lettre que voici.

C : Entrez, s'il vous plaît. Prenez place, monsieur. Veuillez[2] m'excuser. Je vais avertir[3] mon père. *(Elle rentre dans le salon.)*

A : Qui est-ce?

C : C'est un jeune homme. Il t'apporte cette lettre.

B : Qu'est-ce que c'est?

A *(lisant)*: C'est une lettre de recommandation. Mon ami Gaston de New York m'envoie un jeune Américain qui vient à Paris pour étudier[4] la musique. *(Il se lève et va au vestibule.)*

A : Bonjour, monsieur. Les amis de mes amis sont aussi mes amis. Ne voulez-vous pas retirer[5] votre pardessus?

D : Est-ce que je ne vous dérange[6] pas?

A : Pas du tout. Y a-t-il longtemps[7] que vous êtes à Paris?

D : Je viens[8] d'arriver.

A : Allons au salon. *(Ils y vont.)* Je vous présente Monsieur Walton. *(À Charles)* Ma femme . . . ma fille.

B:⎫
C:⎬ Enchantée.

D : Heureux[9] de faire votre connaissance,[10] mesdames.

A *(lui offrant des cigarettes)*: Vous fumez?

D *(prenant une cigarette)*: Oui, merci.

A : Prendrez-vous un verre de porto?[11]

D : Bien volontiers.

B : Nous ferez[12]-vous le plaisir de dîner ici ce soir?

D : Je regrette beaucoup, mais un de mes amis a retenu[13] des places pour l'Opéra et nous dînons également[14] en ville.

---

1 pourrais-je? *could I?*
2 veuillez, *would you please.*
3 avertir, *to inform.*
4 étudier, *to study.*
5 retirer, *to take off.*
6 déranger, *to disturb.*
7 *a long time.*

8 je viens de, *I have just.*
9 heureux, -se, *happy, pleased.*
10 la connaissance, *acquaintance.*
11 *port wine.*
12 *future of* faire.
13 retenir, *to book.*
14 *also, likewise.*

B : C'est dommage.[1] Mais vous viendrez un autre jour?

D : Avec plaisir.

B : Voyons, aujourd'hui[2] c'est lundi. Demain[3] soir je dois faire une visite. Après-demain,[4] vers[5] sept heures, si cela vous convient?

D : Avec le plus grand plaisir.

A *(apportant la bouteille et des verres)* : C'est du porto blanc. (*Il remplit*[6] *les verres.*) À votre bonne santé.[7]

D : À la vôtre.

[1] c'est dommage, *it is a pity.*
[2] *to-day.*
[3] *to-morrow.*
[4] *the day after to-morrow.*
[5] *towards.*
[6] remplir, *to fill.*
[7] la santé, *health.*

FLUENCY PRACTICE — see pp. 63–66

EXPLANATIONS

1. There are various ways of forming questions in French:

   (*a*)   With *est-ce que* placed in front of a statement, e.g. *Est-ce que vous parlez français?*

   (*b*)   Without *est-ce que,* by voice-pitch alone, e.g. *Vous parlez français?*

   (*c*)   When the subject is a pronoun, by placing the verb in front of the pronoun,[1] e.g. *Parlez-vous français? Parle-t-il anglais? Aime-t-elle le vin blanc? Y a-t-il des oranges?* Notice the '*t*' which is added before *il* and *elle*.

   (*d*)   When the subject is a noun, by placing the noun first, and then the verb followed by the appropriate pronoun, e.g. *Votre frère parle-t-il français? Votre sœur vient-elle avec nous? Ces cigarettes sont-elles bonnes?*

2. There are three verbs only where the present tenses used in connection with *vous* (and two of the corresponding imperatives) do not end in *-ez: vous êtes, vous dites, vous faites.*[2]

[1] *This inverted form is not used with* je *in conversational French, except with auxiliary verbs, e.g.* ai-je, dois-je, *etc.*
[2] *The corresponding imperatives are:* soyez, dites, faites.

3. There are four verbs only where the present tense used in connection with *ils* or *elles* does not end in *-ent*:

il (elles) | ont, *they have*
          | sont, *they are*
          | vont, *they go*
          | font, *they do*

4. Ordinal numbers are formed by adding *-ième* to the cardinal numbers. There are special forms for 'the first' *(le premier, la première)* and 'the second' *(le second, la seconde)*, but as an alternative to the latter *deuxième* is also used.

With the exception of *premier*, cardinal numbers are used for dates and the titles of popes, emperors and kings.

FLUENCY PRACTICE

1. Je vous dis | de venir plus tard. | *I tell you* | *to come later.*
Il me dit | de le faire maintenant. | *He tells me* | *to do it now.*
Ils nous disent | de ne pas le faire. | *They tell us* | *not to do it.*
Nous leur disons | de ne pas y aller. | *We tell them* | *not to go there.*
Vous me dites | que c'est trop tard. | *You tell me* | *that it is too late.*
Je lui dirai | que c'est impossible. | *I'll tell him* | *that it is impossible.*

2.

Je	fais	du français à l'école.	*I*	*do*	*French at school.*
Tu		de la gymnastique chaque matin.	*You*		*exercises each morning.*
Il	fait	du sport.	*He*	*does*	*sports.*[1]
Elle		du tennis.	*She*		*tennis.*[1]
		du vélo.			*cycling.*[1]
Ils	font	de l'auto.	*They*	*do*	*motoring.*[1]
Elles		la chambre.			*the room.*
Nous faisons		les malles.	*We*		*the packing.*
Vous faites			*You*		
Je ferai			*I'll*		

[1] *i.e., go in for.*

3. Quand êtes-vous né? | *When were you born?*
Je suis né le vingt et un mars. | *I was born on the 21st of March.*
Votre fils, quand est-il né? | *When was your son born?*
Il est né le vingt-deux juin. | *He was born on the 22nd of June.*
Votre fille, quand est-elle née? | *When was your daughter born?*
Elle est née le trente août. | *She was born on the 30th of August.*

4.

	beaucoup / peu		lettres.
Je lis / J'écris		de	livres.
Tu lis / Tu écris	trop / assez		histoires.
Il lit / Elle écrit			poèmes.
Ils lisent / Elles écrivent	bien		romans.
Nous lisons / écrivons	encore	des	
Vous lisez / écrivez	la plupart		
Je lirai / J'écrirai			

	many / few		letters.
I read / I write			books.
You read / You write	too many / enough		stories.
He reads / She writes			poems.
They read / write	very many		novels.
We read / write	still more		
You read / write	most		
I shall read / write			

5.

Nous restons ici	de 7 à 9 heures.
	du 8 au 15 juin.
	du samedi 11 jusqu'au mardi 14.
	jusqu'au 31 mai.
	jusqu'à vendredi prochain.
	jusqu'à la fin de ce mois.
	jusqu'au commencement du mois prochain.
	pour quinze jours.
	pour trois semaines.
	pour six mois.
	jusqu'à lundi matin.
	jusqu'à mardi soir.

We are staying here	from 7 to 9 o'clock.
	from the 8th to the 15th of June.
	from Saturday the 11th until Tuesday the 14th.
	until the 31st of May.
	until next Friday.
	until the end of this month.
	until the beginning of next month.
	for a fortnight.
	for three weeks.
	for six months.
	until Monday morning.
	until Tuesday evening.

6.

French:

				à		
Venez me voir	dimanche	premier	janvier	à	une heure	un quart.
Nous partons	lundi	deux	février		deux heures	et demie.
Je peux vous voir	mardi	trois	mars		trois heures	moins dix.
Il part	mercredi	dix	avril		quatre heures	moins un quart.
Elle arrive	jeudi	onze	mai		cinq heures	
Ils partent	vendredi	vingt	juin		six heures	
Elles arrivent	samedi	trente et un	juillet		sept heures	
Je vous verrai			août		huit heures	
Pouvez-vous venir			septembre		neuf heures	
			octobre		dix heures	
			novembre		onze heures	
			décembre		midi	
					minuit	

d'aujourd'hui en huit	dans la matinée.
de mercredi en quinze	dans l'après-midi.
la semaine prochaine	dans la soirée.

English:

				at		
Come and see me	on Sunday	the 1st	of January	at	one	fifteen.
We leave	on Monday	the 2nd	of February		two	thirty.
I can see you	on Tuesday	the 3rd	of March		three	less ten.[1]
He leaves	on Wednesday	the 10th	of April		four	less a quarter.[2]
She arrives	on Thursday	the 11th	of May		five	
They leave	on Friday	the 20th	of June		six	
They arrive	on Saturday	the 31st	of July		seven	
I shall see you			of August		eight	
Can you come			of September		nine	
			of October		ten	
			of November		eleven	
			of December		noon	
					midnight	

a week from to-day	during the morning.
a fortnight from next Wednesday	during the afternoon.
next week	during the evening.

[1] i.e., ten to.　　[2] i.e., a quarter to.

65

7. QUEL JOUR DE LA SEMAINE EST-CE?

C'est lundi aujourd'hui.
Ce sera mardi demain.
Ce sera mercredi après-demain.
Jeudi nous aurons une leçon de français.
Vendredi nous irons au théâtre.
Samedi nous jouerons au tennis.
Dimanche nous irons à l'église.

WHAT DAY OF THE WEEK IS IT?

It's Monday to-day.
It will be Tuesday to-morrow.
It will be Wednesday the day after to-morrow.
On Thursday we shall have a French lesson.
On Friday we shall go to the theatre.
We shall play tennis on Saturday.
We shall go to church on Sunday.

8. QUELLE DATE SOMMES-NOUS AUJOURD'HUI?

Le premier janvier.
Le deux février.
Le huit mars.
Le treize avril.
Le douze mai.
Le quatorze juin.
Le quinze juillet.
Le seize août.
Le dix-sept septembre.
Le dix-huit octobre.
Le dix-neuf novembre.
Le vingt décembre.

WHAT IS TO-DAY'S DATE?

The 1st of January.
The 2nd of February.
The 8th of March.
The 13th of April.
The 12th of May.
The 14th of June.
The 15th of July.
The 16th of August.
The 17th of September.
The 18th of October.
The 19th of November.
The 20th of December.

9. C'est | son | premier | livre de français.
           | deuxième |
           | troisième |

It is | his | first | French book.
        | her | second |
              | third |

10. Un billet de | première | classe.
                 | deuxième |

A | first | class ticket.
   | second |

Leçon Douze

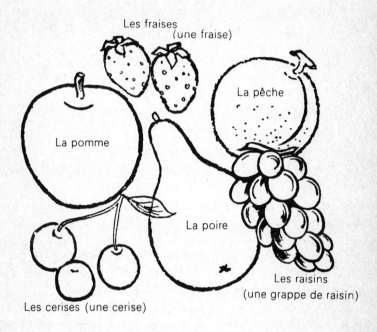

Les fraises (une fraise)

La pêche

La pomme

La poire

Les raisins (une grappe de raisin)

Les cerises (une cerise)

AU MARCHÉ

A : *Mme. Lebrun.*   B : *Mlle. Lebrun.*   C : *La marchande de légumes.*

(Mme. Lebrun et sa fille vont au marché. Le marché a lieu[1] de chaque côté[2] d'une longue rue. Les deux femmes regardent l'étalage[3] d'une marchande[4] de légumes.)

A : Avez-vous des haricots verts?[5]

C : Non, ce n'est pas encore la saison.

A : Y a-t-il des asperges?[6]

---

[1] avoir lieu, *to take place.*
[2] le côté, *side.*
[3] un étalage, *display.*

[4] *dealer* (f.)
[5] les haricots verts, *French beans.*
[6] les asperges *(f. pl.), asparagus.*

C : Oui, il y en a. Regardez, madame, comme elles sont belles.

A : Que coûte cette botte-ci?[1]

C : 1 franc 80.

A : C'est trop cher. Je la prendrai si vous me la laissez[2] pour 1 franc 50.

C : Impossible, madame. C'est le prix de revient.[3] Je vous laisserai celle-ci pour 1 franc 60, parce que[4] vous êtes une bonne cliente.

A : Bien; je la prends. À combien sont les carottes?

C : Trente centimes le kilo.

A : Donnez-m'en un kilo, s'il vous plaît.

C : Et avec ça? Un beau chou-fleur,[5] madame? Regardez comme ils sont beaux!

A : Non, c'est tout pour aujourd'hui. Combien cela fait-il en tout?

C : 1 franc 60 les asperges et 30 centimes les carottes, cela fait 1 franc 90 en tout. *(Mme. Lebrun lui donne deux pièces d'un franc. La marchande lui rend[6] dix centimes.)* Merci bien, madame. Au revoir, madame. Au revoir, mademoiselle.

A *(à sa fille)* : Maintenant pour les fruits. En voilà.

(Elles achètent des fraises* et des cerises.* Ensuite[7] elles traversent la rue pour acheter du beurre, du fromage et des œufs. Quand elles ont fini leurs achats[8] le filet[9] est plein[10] et elles rentrent à la maison.)

---

[1] la botte, *bunch.*
[2] laisser, *to leave, to let have.*
[3] le prix de revient, *cost price.*
[4] parce que, *because.*
[5] le chou-fleur, *cauliflower.*

[6] rendre, *to give back.*
[7] *then, afterwards.*
[8] un achat, *purchase.*
[9] *net, string bag.*
[10] *full.*

FLUENCY PRACTICE

1.						
Donnez	-moi	le billet.	Give	me	the ticket.
Prêtez	-nous	la carte.	Lend	us	the card.
Apportez	-lui	les timbres.	Bring	him (or her)	the stamps.
Envoyez	-leur		Send	them	
Vendez			Sell		

2.

Donnez	-le	-lui!	Give	it (m.)	to him (or her).
Apportez	-la	-leur!	Bring	it (f.)	to them.
Rendez	-les	-moi!	Return	them	to me.
Payez		-nous!	Pay		to us.
Vendez			Sell		
Lisez			Read		

3. Ne

le	lui	donnez	pas!	Don't	give	it (m.)	to him (or her).
la		apportez			bring	it (f.)	to them.
les	leur	rendez			return	them	
		vendez			sell		
		payez			pay		
		lisez			read		

4. Ne

me	le	donnez	pas!	Don't	give	it (m.)	to me.
nous	la	rendez			return	it (f.)	to us.
	les	montrez			show	them	

5. Je (ne)

le	lui	donne	(pas).	I am (not)	giving	it (m.)	to him
la		montre			showing	it (f.)	(or her).
les	leur	prête			lending	them	to them.
		envoie			sending		
		vends			selling		
		rends			returning		
		lis			reading		

6. Il / Elle (ne)

me	le	donne	(pas).
nous	la	montre	
vous	les	prête	
		vend	
		rend	
		lit	

He	is (not)	giving	it (m.)	to me.
She		showing	it (f.)	to us
		lending	them	to you.
		selling		
		returning		
		reading		

7. Ils / Elles (ne)

me	le	donnent	(pas).
nous	la	montrent	
vous	les	prêtent	
		vendent	
		rendent	

They are (not)	giving	it (m.)	to me.
	showing	it (f.)	to us.
	lending		to you.
	selling		
	returning		

8.

Donnons	-le	-lui.	Let us	give	it (m.)	to him (or her).
Payons	-la	-leur.		pay	it (f.)	to them.
Vendons	-les			sell	them	
Rendons				return		
Lisons				read		
Apportons				take		

9. Pourquoi (ne)

me	le	donnez-	vous (pas)?
nous	la	vendez-	
	les	prêtez-	
le	lui	apportez-	
la	leur	payez-	
les		rendez-	

Why do(n't) you	*return*	*it (m.)*	*to me?*
	sell	*it (f.)*	*to us?*
	lend	*them*	
	take		*to him?*
	pay		*to her?*
	return		*to them?*

10. Il m'en donnera.   *He'll give me some.*
Elle vous en apportera.   *She'll bring you some.*
Nous lui en enverrons.   *We'll send him (or her) some.*
Ne leur en montrez pas.   *Don't show them any.*
Est-ce qu'il y en a?   *Are there any?*
Il y en a.   *There are some.*
Il n'y en a pas.   *There aren't any.*

EXPLANATIONS

1. When there are two object pronouns their relative order is as follows:

(*a*)	me	le		(*b*)	le	lui
	te	la			la	leur
	nous	les			les	
	vous					

(*c*) All pronouns precede *y* or *en*. Where both *y* and *en* occur—as in *il y en a*—*y* precedes *en*.

2. The above pronouns precede the verb except in connection with the affirmative imperative, e.g.

   Donnez-le-lui, *give it to him.*

BUT   Ne le lui donnez pas, *don't give it to him.*

3. *Me* changes to *moi* when following a preposition or an imperative, e.g.

   Sans moi, *without me.*
   Suivez-moi, *follow me.*

but not before *en:*

   Donnez-m'en une douzaine, *give me a dozen (of them).*

Note the use of *en* for replacing a noun, where no equivalent word is used in English.

Leçon Treize

Nous avons eu des visites

Les enfants ont joué

Les messieurs ont bu du vin et fumé des cigares

Les dames ont bu du café et mangé des gâteaux

Préparatifs pour le Dîner

A : *Monsieur Lebrun.*   B : *Mme. Lebrun.*   C : *Simone.*
D : *Charles.*

(Mme. Lebrun entre dans la salle à manger, où Simone est en train de[1] mettre la table.[2])

B : As-tu fini, Simone?

C : Pas tout à fait.[3] Où est-ce que je mets ça?

B : Qu'est que c'est?

C : La corbeille à pain.

B : Mets-la sur le buffet[4] pour l'instant. Où as-tu mis le sel[5] et le poivre?[6]

C : Ils sont déjà sur la table.

B : Voyons. Pas comme ça, Simone. Le couteau[7] à droite et la fourchette[8] à gauche.

C : Comme ça, maman?

B : Oui, c'est parfait. As-tu apporté les verres?

C : Je les ai mis[E] sur le buffet.

B : Je vais les mettre[E] sur la table. Tu peux[9] apporter le potage.[10] J'irai chercher[11] les autres.

(Elle met les verres sur la table. Ensuite elle va au salon.)

B : Le dîner est prêt.[12] Allons dans la salle à manger. *(Ils y vont.)*

B *(à Charles)* : Asseyez-vous[13] là, à côté de ma fille.

A : Avez-vous déjà visité le Louvre?

D : Pas encore. Hier j'ai visité le Quartier Latin et cet après-midi j'ai été[14] au Bois de Boulogne. Ce matin j'ai fait quelques achats.[15]

(Simone apporte le potage.)

A : Ah, voilà le potage.

---

[1] être en train de, *to be engaged in.*
[2] mettre la table, *to lay the table.*
[3] tout à fait, *entirely.*
[4] le buffet, *sideboard.*
[5] le sel. *salt.*   [8] la fourchette, *fork.*
[6] le poivre, *pepper.*   [9] tu peux, *you can.*
[7] le couteau, *knife.*   [10] le potage, *soup.*

[11] chercher, *to look for;* aller chercher, *to fetch.*
[12] prêt(e), *ready.*
[13] asseyez-vous, *sit down!*
[14] j'ai été, *I have been.*
[15] faire des achats, *to do shopping* (lit. *to make purchases*).

1. Avez-vous | mangé?   *Have you* | *eaten?*[1]
              | joué? | *played?*
              | bien dormi? | *slept well?*
              | demandé l'addition? | *asked for the bill?*
              | perdu quelque chose? | *lost something?*

2. N'avez-vous pas | bu votre lait?   *Haven't you* | *drunk your milk?*[2]
                 | pris votre bain? | *taken your bath?*
                 | écrit vos lettres? | *written your letters?*
                 | fait une promenade? | *gone for a walk?*
                 | dit cela? | *said that?*
                 | fini ce livre? | *finished this book?*

3.
J'ai	mangé.	*I have*	*eaten.*[3]
Je n'ai pas	joué.	*I have not*	*played.*
Il a	bien dormi.	*He has*	*slept well.*
Il n'a pas	fini le travail.	*He has not*	*finished the work.*
Ils ont	rendu le livre.	*They have*	*returned the book.*
Ils n'ont pas	vendu la maison.	*They have not*	*sold the house.*
Nous avons	été malade.	*We have*	*been ill.*
Nous n'avons pas	eu un accident.	*We have not*	*had an accident.*
	appris le français.		*learned French.*
	compris cela.		*understood that.*

4.
L'ai-je	payé(e)?	*Have I*	*paid for*	*it?*
L'avez-vous	acheté(e)?	*Have you*	*bought*	
L'a-t-il	fini(e)?	*Has he*	*finished*	
L'a-t-elle	vu(e)?	*Has she*	*seen*	
L'ont-ils	pris(e)?	*Have they (*m.*)*	*taken*	
L'ont-elles		*Have they (*f.*)*		

5.
Les ai-je	vendu(e)s?	*Have I*	*sold*	*them?*
Les avez-vous	fini(e)s?	*Have you*	*finished*	
Les a-t-il	vu(e)s?	*Has he*	*seen*	
Les a-t-elle	payé(e)s?	*Has she*	*paid for*	
Les ont-ils	pris(es)?	*Have they (*m.*)*	*taken*	
Les ont-elles	écrit(e)s?	*Have they (*f.*)*	*written*	

6.
Je l'ai	trouvé(e).	*I have*	*found*	*it.*
Je ne l'ai pas	cherché(e).	*I haven't*	*looked for*	*her.*
Elle l'a	vu(e).	*She has*	*seen*	*him.*
Elle ne l'a pas	attendu(e).	*She hasn't*	*waited for*	
Ils l'ont	aidé(e).	*They (*m.*) have*	*helped*	
Ils ne l'ont pas	demandé(e).	*They (*m.*) haven't*	*asked for*	
Elles l'ont	perdu(e).	*They (*f.*) have*	*lost*	

---

[1] or *did you eat, play, etc.*
[2] or *didn't you drink, etc.*
[3] or *I ate, played, slept, etc.*

7.

Je les ai	acheté(e)s.	I have	bought	them.
Je ne les ai pas	vendu(e)s.	I haven't	sold	
Il les a	invité(e)s.	He has	invited	
Il ne les a pas	attendu(e)s.	He hasn't	expected	
Ils les ont	lu(e)s.	They (m.) have	read	
Ils ne les ont pas	oublié(e)s.	They (m.) haven't	forgotten	

8.

Lui	avez-vous	parlé?	Did	you	speak to	him (or her)?
Leur	a-t-il	écrit?		he	write to	them?
	a-t-elle	répondu?		she	answer	
	ont-ils	demandé?		they	ask	
	ont-elles					

9.

Je	lui	ai	parlé.	I	spoke to	him (or her).
	leur		écrit.		wrote to	them.
			répondu.		answered	
			demandé.		asked	

10.

Qu'est-ce que vous avez fait hier?	What did you do yesterday?
J'ai lu toutes mes lettres et j'y ai répondu.	I read all my letters and I replied to them.
Avez-vous écrit beaucoup de lettres?	Did you write many letters?
J'en ai écrit une douzaine, à peu près.	I wrote a dozen (of them) approximately.
Avez-vous bien dîné?	Did you have a good dinner?
J'ai eu un très bon dîner.	I had a very good dinner.
D'abord une salade de tomates.	First a tomato salad.
Ensuite une côtelette de mouton, suivie de haricots verts.	Then a mutton chop, followed by French beans.
Comme dessert une compote de poires.	For dessert stewed pears.
Pour le déjeuner j'ai acheté des petits pains, cent grammes de jambon, des pêches et une bouteille de cidre.	For lunch I bought some rolls, 100 grammes of ham, peaches and a bottle of cider.
Où avez-vous acheté tout cela? Les petits pains? Je les ai achetés chez le boulanger en face de l'hôtel.	Where did you buy all that? The rolls? I bought them at the baker's opposite the hotel.
Le jambon? Je l'ai acheté chez le charcutier au bout de la rue.	The ham? I bought it at the pork butcher's at the end of the street.
Le cidre chez le marchand de vin au coin de la rue, et les pêches au marché sur la grand'place.	The cider at the wine shop at the corner, and the peaches in the market in the main square.
Avez-vous acheté quelque chose chez le boucher? Non, je n y ai rien acheté.	Did you buy anything at the butcher's? No, I didn't buy anything there.

EXPLANATIONS

1. Most happenings in the past are expressed by placing the present tense of *avoir (j'ai, tu as,* etc.) in front of the Past Participle. This tense of the verb is called the Perfect and in French the *Passé Composé.*

74

The endings of the past participle are:

> -é for all verbs ending in -er.
> -i for most verbs ending in -ir.
> -u for most verbs ending in -re or -oir.

The following verbs, amongst others, are irregular:

INFINITIVE	PAST PARTICIPLE
prendre	pris
mettre	mis
dire	dit
écrire	écrit
lire	lu
boire	bu
faire	fait
avoir	eu
être	été

2. The *Passé Composé* not only expresses what has just happened, but also what happened in the past. *Avez-vous . . . ?* followed by the past participle, therefore, is the usual translation not only for 'have you . . . ?' but also for 'did you . . .?'

3. *tout* (pronounced *too*) = 'all', meaning 'everything', 'entirely'.
tous (with sharp *s*) = 'all', meaning 'everybody.'
tous (pronounced *too*) = 'all', followed by a masculine noun,
   e.g. tous les hommes, *all men.*
toutes (pronounced *toot*) = 'all', followed by a feminine noun,
   e.g. toutes les femmes, *all women.*

4. aller chercher, *to fetch,* e.g.:
Allez chercher le médecin, *go and fetch the doctor.*
Envoyez chercher un taxi, *send for a taxi.*

5. *Ne* preceding the verb and *rien* following it = 'nothing', 'not anything'.

6. Note that *y* (like *en*) precedes the verb (except the affirmative form of the imperative—see page 79, 7) or, when the verb is in a compound form, the auxiliary verb.

Leçon Quatorze

Il monte sur le pommier

Il est monté sur le pommier

Il tombe de l'arbre

Il est tombé de l'arbre

LE DÎNER

A : *Monsieur Lebrun.*   B : *Madame Lebrun.*   C : *Simone.*
D : *Charles.*

B : Encore un peu de cette salade?

D : Je veux bien. Elle est excellente.

A : Comment trouvez[1]-vous mon Beaujolais?

D : Il est réellement très bon.

[1] trouver, *to find, to like.*

C : Avez-vous déjà été[E] au théâtre à Paris?

D : Je suis allé[E] à l'Opéra.

C : Qu'est-ce que vous avez vu?

D : *La Flûte Enchantée.*

B : Comment l'avez-vous trouvé?

D : C'était magnifique. Malheureusement j'étais en retard.[1] J'ai manqué[2] l'ouverture et je suis arrivé au milieu[3] du premier acte. L'après-midi j'étais à Chantilly aux courses[4] et je suis revenu trop tard.

B : C'est dommage.[5] Si vous voulez, nous vous ferons entendre[6] notre disque[7] de l'ouverture de *La Flûte Enchantée.*

D : Ce serait[8] très aimable à vous. J'aimerais[9] bien l'entendre.

B *(à Simone)* : Veux-tu[10] enlever[11] les assiettes[12] et apporter le dessert.

A : Qu'est-ce qu'il y a comme dessert?

B : Des fraises avec de la crème fouettée.[13] *(Simone arrive avec le dessert.)*

C : Le voilà. *(Elle sert[14] chaque personne, sauf[15] Gaston.)* Tu as eu ta portion. C'est lui qui a fouetté la crème. Il en a mangé la moitié,[16] le polisson.[17]

D : Je le comprends bien. Il l'a trouvé irrésistible. C'est délicieux. Ne voulez-vous pas lui pardonner?

B : Pour faire plaisir à Monsieur Charles, je te pardonne, petit gourmand.[18] En voilà. *(Elle lui donne une portion.)*

---

[1] en retard, *late.*
[2] manquer, *to miss.*
[3] le milieu, *middle.*
[4] les courses, *races.*
[5] c'est dommage, *it's a pity.*
[6] *to hear.*
[7] le disque, *record.*
[8] *would be.*
[9] *I should like.*

[10] veux-tu, *will you.*
[11] *to take away.*
[12] une assiette, *plate.*
[13] fouetter, *to whip.*
[14] servir, *to serve.*
[15] *except.*
[16] *half.*
[17] *rascal.*
[18] *glutton.*

FLUENCY PRACTICE

1. Êtes-vous | sorti(e)[1] hier? | *Did you* | *go out yesterday?*
   Es-tu | allé(e)[1] au théâtre? | | *go to the theatre?*
   | arrivé(e)[1] ce matin? | | *arrive this morning?*
   | parti(e)[1] hier soir? | | *leave last night?*

2. Je suis | allé(e)[1] | *I have* | *gone[2]*
   Je ne suis pas | sorti(e)[1] | *I haven't* | *gone out*
   Ne suis-je pas | arrivé(e)[1] | *Haven't I* | *arrived*
   Tu es | parti(e)[1] | *You have* | *left*
   Tu n'es pas | monté(e)[1] | *You haven't* | *gone up*
   N'es-tu pas | descendu(e)[1] | *Haven't you* | *gone down*
   Il (elle) est | tombé(e)[1] | *He (she) has* | *fallen*
   Il (elle) n'est pas | | *He (she) hasn't* |
   N'est-il (elle) pas | | *Hasn't he (she)* |

3. Nous sommes | allé(e)s[1] | *We have* | *gone[2]*
   Nous ne sommes pas | sorti(e)s[1] | *We haven't* | *gone out*
   Ne sommes-nous pas | arrivé(e)s[1] | *Haven't we* | *arrived*
   Vous êtes | parti(e)s[1] | *You have* | *left*
   Êtes-vous | monté(e)s[1] | *Have you* | *gone up*
   N'êtes-vous pas | descendu(e)s[1] | *Haven't you* | *gone down*
   Ils (elles) sont | tombé(e)s[1] | *They have* | *fallen*
   Sont-ils (elles) | | *Have they* |
   Ne sont-ils (elles) pas | | *Haven't they* |

4. Y êtes-vous | allé?[1] | *Did you* | *go* | *there?*
   Y es-tu | monté?[1] | | *go up* |
descendu?[1]		*go down*
arrivé?[1]		*arrive*
venu?[1]		*come*

5. J'y | vais. | *I* | *am going* | *there.*
monte.		*am going up*
descends.		*am going down*
arrive.		*am arriving*

6. J'y suis | allé(e). | *I* | *went* | *there.*
monté(e).		*went up*
descendu(e).		*went down*
arrivé(e).		*arrived*

   J'y | allais | souvent. | *I used to* | *go* | *there* | *often.*
   | montais | tous les jours. | | *go up* | | *every day.*
   | descendais | chaque année. | | *go down* | | *each year.*

[1] *Add -e for feminine singular, -s for masculine plural, -es for feminine plural.*
[2] *or I went, etc.*

78

7. Allez-y!   *Go there!*
   Entrez-y!   *Go in there!*
   Montez-y!   *Go up there!*
   Restez-y!   *Stay there!*

N'y	allez	pas!	*Don't*	*go*	*there!*
	entrez			*go in*	
	montez			*go up*	
	restez			*stay*	

8.
Je suis allé	chez	le boulanger	au coin de la rue.
On peut en avoir		le boucher	en face.
Vous pouvez l'acheter		le charcutier	à cent mètres d'ici.
Voulez-vous les acheter		l'épicier	à l'autre bout de la rue.
Je les ai acheté(e)s		le fruitier	près de l'église.
Je les achèterais		le pharmacien	
J'allais		le marchand de	
J'irais		poissons	

I went to	*the baker's*	*at the corner of the street.*
One can get some at	*the butcher's*	*opposite.*
You can buy it at	*the pork butcher's*	*100 metres from here.*
Will you buy them at	*the grocer's*	*at the other end of the street.*
I bought them at	*the greengrocer's*	*near the church.*
I would buy them at	*the chemist's*	
I used to go to	*the fishmonger's*	
I should go to		

9.
J'ai été	à Bruxelles	au printemps.
Nous avons été	à Marseille	en été.
Je suis allé(e)	en Espagne	en automne.
Nous sommes allé(e)s	au Portugal	en hiver.

I was in	*Brussels*	*in spring.*
We were in	*Marseilles*	*in summer.*
I went to	*Spain*	*in autumn.*
We went to	*Portugal*	*in winter.*

10. APPRENEZ PAR CŒUR   LEARN BY HEART

Qu'est ce que c'est que ça?	*What is that?*
Qu'est-ce que ça veut dire?	*What does that mean?*
Ça, ce n'est rien.	*That's nothing.*
Qu'est-ce que c'est que ce bâtiment-là?	*What is that building?*
Ça, c'est le bureau de poste.	*That is the post-office.*
C'est ça.	*That's right—so it is.*
C'est vrai, n'est-ce pas?	*It's true, isn't it?*
Je crois que oui.	*I think so.*
Je crois que non.	*I don't think so.*
J'en suis sûr.	*I am sure of it.*
Je n'en suis pas tout à fait sûr.	*I am not quite sure of it.*

79

1. Verbs denoting motion from one place to another express past happenings with *être*. *Êtes-vous* . . . ? therefore is the usual translation of 'have you . . . ?' or 'did you . . . ?' in connection with *allé, venu, monté, arrivé, entré, sorti, parti, descendu, tombé,* etc. [1]

2. Descriptions, habitual and repeated actions in the past are expressed by the *Imparfait*. The endings of the *Imparfait* are as shown below and there are no exceptions.

je (tu) donnais	je (tu) finissais	je (tu) vendais
il donnait	il finissait	il vendait
ils donnaient	ils finissaient	ils vendaient
nous donnions	nous finissions	nous vendions
vous donniez	vous finissiez	vous vendiez

3. The *Conditionnel* (I should give, etc.) is expressed by the same endings as the *Imparfait,* which are added to the Infinitive, e.g.

je (tu) donnerais	je (tu) finirais	je (tu) vendrais [2]
il donnerait	il finirait	il vendrait
ils donneraient	ils finiraient	ils vendraient
nous donnerions	nous finirions	nous vendrions
vous donneriez	vous finiriez	vous vendriez

The *Conditionnel* of *avoir* is *j'aurais;* of *être, je serais,* etc.

4. The regular conjugation of verbs ending in *-ir* is as for *finir,* to finish.

Present tense: *je finis, tu finis, il finit, ils finissent, nous finissons, vous finissez.* Future: *je finirai, tu finiras,* etc. Imperative: *finis* (fam.), *finissons, finissez.* Imperfect and Conditional: see above. Past Participle: *fini.* Note that an extra syllable *-iss-* is added to the stem of the verb in the plural forms of the present tense, the corresponding forms of the imperative, and to all forms of the imperfect.

---

[1] *also* je suis resté, *I stayed;* je suis né, *I was born;* il est mort, *he died; but* j'ai couru, *I ran;* j'ai marché, *I walked;* j'ai nagé, *I swam.*

[2] *Note that the verbs whose infinitive ends in* -re *drop the* e *when forming the* Conditionnel.

Leçon Quinze

Il dort

Il se réveille

Il se lève

Il s'habille

Le Lever

A : *Monsieur Lebrun.*   B : *Madame Lebrun.*   C : *Simone.*
D : *Gaston.*

(Il est sept heures du matin. Mme. Lebrun se lève. Monsieur Lebrun
se réveille. Simone et Gaston dorment encore.)*

B : As-tu bien dormi?[1]

A : Oui, chéri. Et toi?

B : Pas trop bien. La radio des voisins[2] m'a empêchée[3] de m'endormir[4] avant deux heures.

A : Je parlerai à la concierge. Maintenant je vais me raser.[5]

B : N'oublie pas de réveiller[6] les enfants!

[1] dormir, *to sleep*
[2] le voisin, *the neighbour.*
[3] empêcher, *to prevent.*
[4] s'endormir, *to fall asleep.*
[5] se raser, *to shave.*
[6] *to wake.*

A *(frappant aux portes des chambres de Simone et de Gaston)*: Levez-vous, mes enfants. Il est sept heures.

(Simone se lève immédiatement, mais Gaston reste au lit. Quelques minutes plus tard sa sœur vient dans sa chambre.)

C : Quoi! Tu n'es pas encore levé? Lève-toi immédiatement.

D : Laisse-moi dormir encore cinq minutes. J'ai tellement sommeil.[1] Je ne peux pas me lever.

C : Pas de mauvaises excuses. Il est temps de se lever. Est-ce que que tu te lèves? Oui ou non? Je compte[2] jusqu'à trois: un, deux, trois. *(Elle lui retire la couverture.[3])*

D : Laisse[4]-moi tranquille.[5]

C *(se sauvant[6])*: N'oublie pas de te laver le cou[7] comme d'habitude.[8]

(Gaston lui jette[9] un oreiller[10] sans la toucher. Il le ramasse[11] et se précipite[12] à la salle de bain où son père est en train de se raser.)

---

[1] avoir sommeil, *to feel sleepy.*
[2] compter, *to count.*
[3] *blanket.*
[4] laisser, *to let, to leave*
[5] *quiet, undisturbed.*
[6] se sauver, *to run away.*
[7] le cou, *neck.*
[8] comme d'habitude, *as usual.*
[9] jeter, *to throw.*
[10] un oreiller, *pillow.*
[11] ramasser, *to pick up.*
[12] se précipiter, *to rush.*

FLUENCY PRACTICE

1. Lève-toi!   *Get up!*
   Levez-vous!
   Réveille-toi!   *Wake up!*
   Réveillez-vous!
   Dépêche-toi!   *Hurry!*
   Dépêchez-vous!
   Ne te brûle pas!   *Don't burn yourself!*
   Ne vous brûlez pas!
   Ne te coupe pas!   *Don't cut yourself!*
   Ne vous coupez pas!
   Ne te lève pas!   *Don't get up!*
   Ne vous levez pas!

2.

Je me	lève.	*I am*	*getting up.*
Il se	lave.	*He is*	*washing.*
Elle se	promène.	*She is*	*going for a walk.*
	couche.		*going to bed.*

Ils se	lèvent de bonne heure.	*They are*	*getting up early.*
Elles se	couchent tard.		*going to bed late.*
	lavent les mains.		*washing their hands.*

Nous nous	habillons. déshabillons. couchons.		We are	getting dressed. getting undressed. going to bed.	
Est-ce que vous vous	levez? reposez? dépêchez?		Are you	getting up? resting? hurrying?	

3. Levons-nous! — *Let us get up!*
   Dépêchons-nous! *Let us hurry!*
   Reposons-nous! *Let us have a rest!*
   Amusons-nous! *Let us enjoy ourselves!*
   Ne nous levons pas! *Don't let us get up!*
   Ne nous couchons pas encore! *Don't let us go to bed yet!*

4.
Je ne me Il ne se Elle ne se	lève couche	pas.	I am not He is not She is not	getting up. going to bed.	
Ne te	lèves-tu couches-tu	pas?	Aren't you	getting up? going to bed?	
Nous ne nous	habillons déshabillons	pas.	We are not	dressing. undressing.	
Vous ne vous	réveillez dépêchez	pas. jamais.	You	don't never	wake up. hurry.

5.
Ils Elles	ne	se trompent se lavent se dépêchent s'amusent	jamais.

They never | *make a mistake.*
wash.
hurry.
enjoy themselves.

6.
Venez avec	moi.	Come with	me.
N'allez pas sans	lui.	Don't go without	him.
Ce n'est pas pour	elle.	It is not for	her.
C'est à	nous.	It belongs to	us.
Ce n'est pas à	eux.	It does not belong to	them (m.).
Ce livre est à	elles.	This book belongs to	them (f.).
Ces livres sont à	vous. toi.	These books belong to	you. you (fam.).

7.
Allons Il n'y a personne Y a-t-il quelqu'un	chez	moi toi lui elle nous vous eux elles	Let's go to There's no one at Is there anyone at	my your his her our your their (m.) their (f.)	place

8. QUI EST LÀ? — WHO IS THERE?

C'est	moi. toi. lui. elle. nous. vous.	It is	I. you (fam.). he. she. we. you.
Ce sont	eux. elles.		they (m.). they (f.).

9. Comment vous appelez-vous?	*What is your name?*
Je m'appelle Édouard.	*My name is Edward.*
Comment s'appelle votre frère?	*What is your brother's name?*
Il s'appelle Jean.	*His name is John.*
Et votre sœur, comment s'appelle-t-elle?	*And what is your sister called?*
Elle s'appelle Louise.	*Her name is Louise.*

EXPLANATIONS

1. *Laver* = to wash, in the sense of to do some washing or to wash somebody, e.g.

> Je lave ma petite sœur, *I wash my little sister.*
> Il lave ses chaussettes, *he washes his socks.*
> se laver, *to wash oneself.*

A verb where the same person is both the subject and the object of the action is called a reflexive verb.

The reflexive pronouns are:

> me, *myself.*
> te, *yourself (fam.).*
> se, *himself, herself, itself, oneself, themselves.*
> nous, *ourselves.*
> vous, *yourself, yourselves.*

Note from the examples given in the Fluency Practice section that some verbs are reflexive in French which are not so in English.

2. *Ne* preceding the verb and *jamais* following it means 'never'.

3. The pronouns *je, te, me, se, le, il* and *ils,* can only be used in connection with verbs. They are called 'weak' pronouns, because they cannot stand by themselves.

The following so-called 'strong' or 'stressed' pronouns, take their place when used after prepositions and after *c'est* or *ce sont*:

> moi, *for both 'I' and 'me',*
> lui, *for both 'he' and 'him',*
> soi, *for 'oneself',*
> eux, *for both 'they' and 'them' (m.),*
> toi, *for 'you' in the familiar form.*

Strong pronouns can also be used with verbs for emphasis and must always be used if there is no verb, e.g. *Qui est là?—Moi!*
See also Lesson XII, Note 3.

84

Leçon Seize

UN RENDEZ-VOUS

C : *Charles.*   S : *Simone.*

(Quelques jours après le dîner chez les Lebrun, nous voyons Charles dans sa chambre. Il s'est levé de bonne heure[1] et il a déjà pris le petit déjeuner. Après avoir[2] trouvé le numéro des Lebrun dans l'annuaire[3] téléphonique il s'approche de l'appareil, décroche[4] le récepteur[5] et compose le numéro.)

C : Allô. C'est bien le 157-08-63? Ai-je le plaisir de parler à Mademoiselle Lebrun?

S : Oui, c'est bien moi. Qui est à l'appareil?

C : C'est moi, Charles. Bonjour, mademoiselle, comment allez-vous?

S : Très bien. Et vous?

C : Plutôt[6] mal. Je me sens[7] si seul.[8]

S : Pauvre Charles. Venez nous voir.

C : Je voudrais bien.[9] Mais il fait si beau,[10] il vaut mieux[11] aller se promener en plein air.[12]

S : Je suis tellement occupée. J'ai mes cours à suivre.[13] À onze heures j'aurai une leçon d'anglais.

C : Eh bien, nous parlerons anglais tout le temps. Ce sera plus utile[14] pour vous que de suivre des leçons.

S : N'êtes-vous pas venu à Paris pour apprendre[15] le français?

C : C'est exact. Mais nous pourrions parler anglais la moitié du temps et français ensuite.

S : C'est une bonne idée!

---

[1] de bonne heure, *early.*
[2] après avoir, *after having.*
[3] un annuaire, *directory.*
[4] décrocher, *to unhook.*
[5] *receiver.*
[6] *rather.*
[7] se sentir, *to feel.*
[8] *alone.*
[9] je voudrais bien, *I should like to.*

[10] il fait si beau, *it is such a fine day.*
[11] il vaut mieux, *it is better to (from valoir, to be worth).*
[12] le plein air, *the open air.*
[13] suivre des cours, *to attend (lit. to follow) classes.*
[14] *useful.*
[15] *to learn.*

Il fait du soleil
(Elle prend un bain de soleil)

Il fait chaud
(Le monsieur
s'essuie le front)

Il fait du vent
(Le vent a emporté son
chapeau. Elle court
l'attraper)

Il fait froid
(La petite fille se
frotte les mains)

Il pleut
(Le monsieur
ouvre son
parapluie)

Il neige
(Les enfants jettent des boules
de neige)

C : Je me suis levé de bonne heure pour vous téléphoner avant votre leçon. Ne pouvez-vous pas la décommander?[1]

S : Il est trop tard. Mon professeur est déjà en route.[2] Mais je serai libre cet après-midi. Venez me chercher à trois heures. Je demanderai à maman de venir, si vous voulez bien. Elle ne s'est pas sentie très bien ce matin. Le plein air lui fera du bien.

C : Entendu.[3] Je viendrai à trois heures. À tout à l'heure. (*Il raccroche le récepteur en disant:*) Zut![4] Pas de chance![5]

[1] *to cancel*
[2] en route, *on the way.*
[3] *agreed.*
[4] *a mild exclamation, expressing anger or disappointment.*
[5] pas de chance, *no luck.*

FLUENCY PRACTICE

1. Je me suis

lavé(e).	*I washed myself.*
rasé(e).	*I shaved myself.*
habillé(e).	*I dressed myself.*
levé(e).	*I got up.*
couché(e).	*I went to bed.*
enrhumé(e).	*I caught a cold.*

2. Vous êtes-vous / T'es-tu

lavé(e)?	*Did you*	*wash yourself?*
rasé?		*shave yourself?*
coupé(e)?		*cut yourself?*
brûlé(e)?		*burn yourself?*
levé(e)?		*get up?*

3.

Il s'est	levé(e)	*He has*	*got up*
Elle s'est	lavé(e)	*She has*	*washed*
S'est-il	habillé(e)	*Has he*	*dressed*
S'est-elle	déshabillé(e)	*Has she*	*undressed*
Il ne s'est pas	coupé(e)	*He hasn't*	*cut himself (herself)*
Elle ne s'est pas	brûlé(e)	*She hasn't*	*burnt herself (himself)*
Ne s'est-il pas	reposé(e)	*Hasn't he*	*had a rest*
Ne s'est-elle pas	couché(e)	*Hasn't she*	*laid down*

4.

Nous nous sommes	réveillé(e)s	*We have*	*woken up*
Nous sommes-nous	levé(e)s	*Have we*	*got up*
	lavé(e)s		*washed*
Nous ne nous sommes pas	habillé(e)s	*We haven't*	*dressed*
Ne nous sommes-nous pas	dépêché(e)s	*Haven't we*	*hurried*

5.

Vous vous êtes	brûlé(e)s	*You have*	*burnt yourselves*
Vous êtes-vous	coupé(e)s	*Have you*	*cut yourselves*
	déshabillé(e)s		*undressed*
Vous ne vous êtes pas	reposé(e)s	*You haven't*	*had a rest*
Ne vous êtes-vous pas	couché(e)s	*Haven't you*	*gone to bed*

6.

Ils se sont	levé(e)s de bonne heure
Elles se sont	habillé(e)s vite
Se sont-ils	promené(e)s dans le parc
Se sont-elles	deshabillé(e)s à la plage
Ils ne se sont pas	coupé(e)s
Elles ne se sont pas	embarqué(e)s sur un voilier
Ne se sont-ils pas	bien amusé(e)s
Ne se sont-elles pas	reposé(e)s

They have (m.)	got up early
They have (f.)	dressed quickly
Have they (m.)	gone for a walk in the park
Have they (f.)	undressed on the beach
They haven't (m.)	cut themselves
They haven't (f.)	embarked on a sailing boat
Haven't they (m.)	enjoyed themselves
Haven't they (f.)	had a rest

7.

Je me suis			I	
	coupé la main.			cut my hand.
	brûlé la langue.			burned my tongue.
	foulé la cheville.			sprained my ankle.
	fait mal à la jambe.			hurt my leg.

8.

Qu'avez-vous?	What is the matter with you?
Qu'a-t-il?	What is the matter with him?
Qu'ont-ils?	What is the matter with them?
Vous êtes-vous fait mal?	Have you hurt yourself?

9. OÙ AVEZ-VOUS MAL?   WHERE DOES IT HURT?

J'ai mal			I have	
	à la gorge.			a sore throat.
	aux dents.			toothache.
	à la tête.			a headache.
	à l'estomac.			a stomach-ache.
	à la jambe.			a sore leg.
	au pied.			a sore foot.
	au doigt.			a sore finger.
	à l'œil.			a sore eye.
	à l'oreille.			a sore ear.
	au genou.			a bad knee.

10.

A quelle heure vous êtes-vous levé ce matin?	What time did you get up this morning?
Ne vous êtes-vous pas couché tard hier?	Didn't you go to bed late yesterday?
Où êtes-vous allé?	Where did you go?
N'êtes-vous pas allé au théâtre?	Didn't you go to the theatre?
Nous sommes allés au cinéma.	We went to the cinema.
Qu'est-ce que vous avez vu?	What did you see?
Avez-vous eu une bonne place?	Did you have a good seat?
Vous êtes-vous bien amusés?	Did you enjoy yourselves?

1. Reflexive verbs (see Lesson XV) form their *Passé Composé* with *être*. *Vous êtes-vous . . . ?* therefore, is the usual translation for 'did you . . . ?' or 'have you . . . ?' in connection with reflexive verbs. The corresponding familiar form is *t'es-tu . . . ?*

2. Note the present tense of the verbs *dormir*, to sleep; *mentir*, to lie; *sortir*, to go out; *servir*, to serve; *partir*, to leave; *sentir*, to feel (to be aware of), to smell; *courir*, to run:

je	dors	il	dort	ils	dorment	nous	dormons	vous	dormez
tu	mens	elle	ment	elles	mentent		mentons		mentez
	sors		sort		sortent		sortons		sortez
	sers		sert		servent		servons		servez
	pars		part		partent		partons		partez
	sens		sent		sentent		sentons		sentez
	cours		court		courent		courons		courez

3. Some reflexive verbs derived from the above are *s'endormir*, to fall asleep; *se servir*, to help oneself; *se sentir*, to feel (well, ill, tired, etc.).

4. The *Passé Composé* of the above verbs is:

j'ai	dormi[1]	je suis	sorti[2]	je me suis	endormi[2]
tu as	menti	tu es	parti[2]	tu t'es	servi[2]
il a	servi	il est		il s'est	senti
ils ont	senti	ils sont		ils se sont	
nous avons	couru	nous sommes		nous nous sommes	
vous avez		vous êtes		vous vous êtes	

[1] *Past participles used in connection with* avoir *remain unchanged unless a direct object precedes, e.g.* Elles ont bien dormi, *but* Les sardines? Nous les avons achetées.

[2] *Add* -e *for the feminine,* -s *for the masculine plural,* -es *for the feminine plural.*

5. *A* means 'in', 'at' or 'to'. With the names of countries, most of which are feminine, *en* is used for both 'in' and 'to'. Some countries are masculine and use *à*, e.g. *au Japon, au Maroc, au Portugal, aux États-Unis* (United States).

PRONUNCIATION AND SPELLING
Vowels

SOUND[1]	USUAL SPELLING	OTHER SPELLINGS	EXAMPLES
No. 1	i	î, y	si, île, cycle
No. 2	é	final -ez, -er, and -ai in verbal endings	blé, été, donné, donnez, manger, j'irai, j'ai
No. 3	è, ê, ai, ei, ay	e followed by two consonants,[2] or between consonants in words of one syllable[3]	père, français, fête, reine, crayon, elle, chef, sel
No. 4	a	à	madame, là
No. 5	â	a in words ending in -as(se) or ail(le)[4]	âge, las, tasse, bétail, bataille
No. 6	o	au followed by hard g, l, r, sc, st, sp	col, robe, Paul, Auguste, auspice
No. 7	ô, eau	o, au when followed by a silent consonant at the end of a word, by soft s or sse	hôtel, beau, trop, haut, rose, oser, gros, grosse, faux, fausse
No. 8	ou, oû, où	aoû, in août, August	route, goût
No. 9	u, û	il eut, vous eûtes, ils eurent, eu (the past participle of avoir)	vu, sûr, lue
No. 10	eu, eû	œu when followed by a silent consonant at the end of a word	feu, deux, nœud, jeûne (the fast)

[1] For the description of sounds, see pages 9–12.
[2] *Like sound No. 2 when followed by* ff (effort, effet, effectif, *etc.*), *also in the word* et.
[3] *Also when the first letter in a syllable* (cruel), *and final* -et (complet, billet, *etc.*)
[4] *For the pronunciation of* ail(le), *see page* 12.

No. 11	œu	eu, when followed by a sounded consonant, other than s, at the end of a word[1]	sœur, bœuf, neuf, jeune (young)
No. 12	e[2]	ai in faisons, faisant and the first ai in je faisais, etc.	le, me, se, te, bre-bis, reçu
No. 13	on, om		bon, vont, nom
No. 14	an, am en, em	ean, aen, aon	an, lampe, enfant, temps, Jean, Caen, paon
No. 15	in, im ain, aim	ein, eim, yn, ym[3]	vin, pain, faim, simple, plein, Reims, larynx, sympathie
No. 16	un, um	eun in à jeun ('on an empty stomach')	un, brun, parfum

[1] *In words ending in -euse or -eutre the eu has sound No. 10 (chanteuse, neutre), as does meule (millstone).*

[2] *Silent when final in words of more than one syllable, and also between two consonants which can be pronounced easily without it (la fenêtre, le boulevard, le médecin), even between words as in ce n'est pas vrai; also in the verbal ending -ent (ils marchent).*

[3] *Also -en in moyen, examen, appendice, benzine, Rubens, européen, bien, combien and other words ending in -ien.*

NOTES

(1) *Whenever a vowel is followed by m or n it becomes a nasal. Nasals are vowel sounds and it makes no difference to their pronunciation whether m or n follows. If the m or n is doubled or followed by a vowel, or h, there is no nasal sound and the m or n is pronounced as a consonant (e.g.* animal, bonheur, brune, homme, bonne).

(2) *No nasal sounds are used in the following foreign words:*
    Sound No. 3: amen, Harlem, Jérusalem, *and a few others.*
    Sound No. 4: Islam, Wagram, Abraham.
    Sound No. 6: album, opium, minimum, maximum, ultimatum, *and a few others.*

(3) *The following words have sound No. 4:* la femme, solennel, fréquemment *and other words ending in -emment.*

(4) *Initial* en-, *although followed by a vowel, is nasal in* enivrer, enamourer, enorgueiller, *and a few others.*

(5) *Initial* enn- *and* emm- *are nasal:* ennui, ennuyer, emmener, *but not* ennemi.

Vowels may be short or long in pronunciation, but it is difficult to give hard and fast rules which cover all cases. For instance, vowel sound No. 3 is short in *mettre*, but the same sound is long in *maître*; in this case the difference is indicated by the circumflex accent on the latter, but there are no indications at all to show the difference between, for instance, the short *a* in *la chasse* and the long *a* in *la tasse*.

In general it is preferable to keep all vowels *short*. However, a vowel sound at the end of a word is *long* in the following cases:

(*a*) if followed by *-ge, -ve, -z, -ze, -s* having the sound of *z*, a sounded *-r*:

> *sage, cave, gaz, gaze, rose, jour, père, alors*

(*b*) in words where a single *l* or a double *ll* have the sound of *y*:

> *travail, paille, abeille, soleil, famille, fauteuil, feuille, grenouille*

(*c*) a nasal vowel sound is long when followed by a consonant and *-e*:

> *jambe, pente, quinze, bonde, emprunte.*

CONSONANTS

For the pronunciation of *b, p, m, v, f,* see page 13.

c	as in **c**ool:	
	(1) before *a, o, u*	*café, col, curé, cousin*
	(2) before a consonant	*classe, cloche, craie, correct*
	(3) at the end of a word	*chic, sec, grec, lac, truc*
	as in ri**c**e before *e, i, y*	*ce, ceci, civil, cygne*
ç	always as in ri**c**e	*ça, français, garçon, leçon*
cc	like **k** before *a, o, u,* or a consonant	*accuser, accordéon, accumulateur, acclimatation, accroissement*
	like **ks** before *e* or *i*	*accent, accident, successeur*

ch	like English **sh**	*chou, chef, mouchoir*
	like **k** in foreign words	*écho, Christ, chrétien, chœur, choléra, Munich, orchestre, chronomètre, technique, archéologie, chrysanthème, orchidée*
g	as in **g**o before *a, o, u,* or a consonant (other than *n*)	*gant, wagon, légumes, gris, grand, groupe, glace*
	before *e, i, y,* soft as the **s** in pleasure	*génie, magie, gymnastique*
ge	soft as above in the combinations *gea* and *geo* (the *e* is mute here and merely serves as an indication that the *g* is soft)	*le geai, nous mangeons, Georges, je mangeais*
gu[1]	like hard **g** (the *u* is mute here and merely serves as an indication that the *g* is hard)	*langue, guerre, guitare, anguille*
gn	like the part in heavy type of ca**ny**on	*signe, signal, Bretagne, Allemágne, oignon*[2]
h	Although in modern French *h* is always silent, the following difference is made:	
	(1) *h muet:*	
	Most words beginning with *h* are treated as if they began with a vowel, i.e. the article before the noun becomes *l'* and there is liaison between a preceding final consonant and the vowel following the *h*	*l'habit, l'herbe, l'hiver, l'histoire, une femme honnête, un homme heureux, un conte historique*
	(2) *h aspiré:*	
	This was sounded in former times and is still treated as if it were a consonant, i.e. there is	*la hache, le hachis, les Halles, le hareng, le haricot, le hasard, la Hollande, la Hongrie, le*

[1] *The u is sounded in* l'aiguille, *needle,* which is pronounced *aig-weey.*

[2] *Pronounced* o-nyon.

93

	neither liaison nor elision in the examples given and a few other words	*hors-d'œuvre, haut, le héros, la harpe*
j	like soft **g** (i.e. like the *s* in mea*s*ure)	*jamais, journal, jalousie*
l[1]	as in English lamp, never as in English 'all'	*lampe, livre, fil, cheval*
ll[2]	like single **l**	*balle, salle, ballon, illustré*
q, qu	like **k**	*le coq, cinq, cinquante, quinze, quand, quatre, qualité*
	Note.—*qu* is pronounced as in English **qu**ality in the five words opposite	*quadruple, aquarium, aquatique, aquarelle, équateur*
r	Of the various *r* sounds used by different French speakers we recommend the so-called uvular *r*, which is the most commonly used. It is produced at the back of the mouth (like the hard *g*) and may be practised by saying repeatedly: *gand, grand; gain, grain; gond, grond.* It is, in fact, the same sound we produce repeatedly when gargling and, therefore, not difficult to acquire	*rond, rose, rouge, rincer, ragoût, livre, théâtre, montre, verre, verte, noir*
s	at the beginning of a word and when preceded or followed by a consonant, sharp as in the English word sea	*son, sans, sac, penser, tester*
	between vowels, soft as in English rose	*rose, chaise, musique*
	Note.—*s* is soft in the following words, although preceded by a consonant	*Alsace, transaction, transition, transatlantique*

[1] *For the pronunciation of* il *after a preceding vowel, see page* 12.
[2] *For the pronunciation of* ill, *see page* 12.

ss	like sharp **s**	*poisson, assassin, chasse*
sc	as in English **sc**andal before *a, o, u,* or a consonant	*scandale, sculpture, scrutin*
	as in English **sc**ience before *e, i, y*	*sceptre, science, scène, scylla, descendre*
t	as in English **t**ime, but sharp and terse	*taxi, tigre, portier, moitié, question, digestion*
	like sharp **s** in the endings *-tial, -tience, -tiel, -tieux, -tion* (but not *-stion*), *-tie*[1] (but not *-tié*), also in *balbutier* and the first *t* in *initiative*	*partiel, essentiel, patience, ambitieux, nation, ration, libération, diplomatie, bureaucratie*
th	is pronounced like **t**	*thé, théâtre, théorie, thym*
v w }	like English **v**	*vin, vent, valable, neuve, wagon, wallon, warranter*
x	in the syllable *ex* followed by a vowel or *h*, like the English word **eggs**	*exact, exemple, exercice, examen, exhorter*
	like sharp **s** in *six, dix, soixante, Bruxelles*	
	like **z** in *deuxième, sixième, dixième, deux oranges, six enfants dix hommes* and whenever *deux, dix* and *six* are used in connection with words beginning with a vowel or *h* mute	
	as in English ta**x**i in all cases not mentioned above	*luxe, axe, taxi, extra*
y	followed by a vowel, as in English yes	*le yacht, payer, les yeux, royal, le loyer*
	followed by a consonant, *y* is a vowel (see page 90)	
z	as in English	*zéro, zone, zoologique*

[1] *Except* la sortie.

1. Final unaccented *e* is not sounded, unless it is the only vowel as in *me, se, te, le.*

2. Final consonants are silent, except *c, f, l, q, r,* which are usually sounded.

Exceptions:

b is sounded in foreign words: *club, Jacob.*

c is silent in *tabac, porc, broc* (jug), *estomac* (stomach), *escroc* (crook), *caoutchouc* (rubber), *blanc, banc, franc, respect,* and a few more words.

d is sounded in *sud* (south), and in proper names like *David.*

f is not sounded in *clef* (key), *cerf, les nerfs, les œufs, les bœufs* and *chef-d'œuvre* (masterpiece).

l is silent in *fusil* (rifle), *outil* (tool), *sourcil* (eyebrow), *gentil* (nice), and a few more words.

r is silent in the infinitive ending *-er (aimer, marcher,* etc.), and in the ending *-ier: papier, panier, cahier,* etc. (but the *r* is sounded in *hier* and *fier*).

s is sounded in *autobus, tennis, gratis, jadis, as, mœurs, atlas, terminus, hélas, le sens, le lis, bis, plus* (but silent in *plus que* and *plus de), mars, l'ours, la vis* (screw), *tournevis* (screwdriver), *vasistas* (ventilator), and the singular of *os* (bone).

t is pronounced in *mat, sept, l'est, l'ouest, déficit, tact, strict, exact, huit* (except when followed by a word beginning with a consonant), *Christ* (but *st* is silent in *Jésus-Christ).*

x is sounded in *index, Aix, lynx, larynx* and a few others.

z is sounded in *gaz,* and some foreign words like *fez* and *jazz.*

NOTES

(*a*) Both final letters are silent in *poids* (weight), *corps, pouls. remords, doigt, respect, aspect, instinct, distinct,* but both consonants are sounded in *strict, district, compact, tact, est* (east), *Brest.*

(*b*) If a word ends in three consecutive consonants, the last two are usually silent, e.g. the *ps* in *corps* and *temps,* the *pt* in *exempt* and *prompt,* the *gt* in *vingt,*[1] the *ds* in *prends, vends, attends* and similar verb forms.

[1] t *is sounded in* vingt et un, vingt-deux, vingt-trois, *etc.*

SILENT LETTERS

1. Most final consononts (see 'Final Letters' opposite).

2. Final unaccented *e* in words of more than one syllable (see 'Final Letters').

3. ALSO SILENT ARE:

a in *août* (August) and *Saône* (name of a river).

e in *Caen* (name of a town).

i in *oignon*.

o in *faon* (fawn), *paon* (peacock) and *Laon* (name of a town), which are pronounced as if spelt *fan, pan* and *lan*.

l in *fils*.

m in *automne, damner, condamner*.

p in *sept, bâpteme* (baptism), *sculpteur, sculpture, compter, dompter*.

th in *asthme, asthmatique*.

LIAISON

When a word ending in a consonant (even when it is a silent one) is followed by a word begining with a vowel, the two words are often joined together in pronunciation. This linking of words is called *liaison*, but it only takes place if the two words are closely connected in sense, and if there is no pause between the two words.

It is impossible to give precise rules as to where liaison should or should not take place, as it depends on the rate of speech, on the tone of the speaker and whether the language is conversation, reading aloud or public speaking. There is less liaison in ordinary conversation than in careful and formal speaking.

Liaison is obligatory only in the following cases:

1. Between articles, numerals, pronouns, adjectives and the nouns which follow them, e.g. *les_hommes, huit_enfants, bon_appétit, mon_oncle, ils_ont, ces_oranges, aux_États-Unis*.

2. Between adverb and adjective, or adverb and adverb, e.g. *très_intéressant, bien_aimable, tout_autre*.

3. After prepositions and negative words such as *pas, point, plus, jamais*, e.g. *dans_une minute, en_hiver, chez_eux, sans_elle, pas_encore, plus_un seul*.

4. After auxiliaries, e.g. *ont‿eu, sont‿arrivés, est‿occupé.*

5. In compound words and ready-made phrases, e.g. *tout‿à coup, de temps‿en temps, de plus‿en plus.*

Never use liaison in the following cases:

(*a*) after *et* (and), e.g. *une pomme et une orange.*

(*b*) after the *r* of the infinitive ending -*er*, e.g. *chanter une chanson.*

(*c*) with a mute consonant following a pronounced *r*, e.g. *il sort à une heure, un court intervalle.* (In these two examples you link the *r*, but not the *t*).

(*d*) before *h aspiré*, e.g. *deux homards, Les Halles, les huit jours.*

(*e*) before *onze*, e.g. *le onze avril, les onze gâteaux.*

NOTE. In liaison, final *d* is pronounced *t*, *f* is pronounced *v*, and *s* or *x* like *z*, e.g. *un grand hôtel, deux heures, neuf ans.*

SYLLABIFICATION

The division of words into syllables is different in French and English. The following rules are important because without them it is impossible to know how to pronounce unaccented *e*.

1. A consonant belongs to the following syllable, not the preceding one, e.g. *Me/lun, be/soin, beau/té.*

2. Consecutive consonants are divided between two syllables, e.g. *Ver/dun, ser/pent, pro/tes/tant.*

3. *r* and *l* preceded by other consonants form inseparable groups with these, e.g. *li/vre, peu/ple, tien/drai.*

4. *ch, gn* and *tn* are inseparable, e.g. *a/chat, a/gneau, ca/tho/lique.*

NOTE. There is no nasal sound before *n* or *m* if the vowel (or vowels) belong to different syllables, e.g. *se/maine, a/ni/mal.*

PUNCTUATION

.	point (*m.*)	?	point d'interrogation
,	virgule (*f.*)	-	trait d'union (*m.*)
;	point et virgule	—	tiret (*m.*)
:	deux points	" "	guillemets (*m. pl.*)
!	point d'exclamation	( )	parenthèses (*f. pl.*)

PRONUNCIATION PRACTICE
Vowels

1. si, ri, ni, lit, nid, gris, pris, livre, cidre, fini, il lit six livres.

2. né, dé, blé, thé, été, cédé, bébé, préféré, j'ai, j'irai, nez, clef.[1]

3. père, mère, frère, nègre, règle, lève, grève, tête, fête, bête, mêle, bêche, fenêtre, prêtre, chaise, craie, laine, aime, aide, fraise, chaîne, peine, neige, reine, elle, est, cette, fer, lettre, mettre, terre, billet, complet, objet.

4. rat, chat, quatre, sac, canne, banane, bagage, la dame.

cité, écrit, vérité, église, fidèle, répète, sévère, dictée, animal, madame, cardinal, canif, décrire, fermer, cavité, il est ici, elle est là, il est assis, elle est assise, il est midi, elle a six livres, j'ai donné les clefs au bébé.

5. âme, âge, tâche, câble, âne, Pâques.

6. col, robe, porte, coq, homme, cloche, botte, bonne, pomme, notre.

7. tôt, côte, cône, dôme, drôle, tôle, pôle, rôle, jaune, sauf, sauce, gauche, auto, aubergine, beau, seau, tableau, gâteau, chapeau, bateau.

8. nous, vous, tout, rouge, jour, cour, four, blouse, coucou.

joli, poli, politesse, honnête, bonnet, beauté, goûté, fâché, automobile, moutarde, foulard, bouleau, oublié, boulette, ouvrir, ouvert, couvert, souffert, freiné, frisé, fourré, hibou, rideau, drapeau, plateau, corbeau, morceau, couteau.

la robe est jolie, Rosalie tricote, Papa dort, Victor part pour la gare, il fait beau, il fait chaud, il n'a pas fini sa tâche.

9. bu, tu, vu, lu, mur, dur, une, brune, lune, lutte, plume, fume, futur.

10. peu, feu, bleu, jeu, yeux, Dieu, queue, pneu, furieux, nœud, vœux.

---

[1] also spelt *clé*.

99

11. œuf, bœuf, sœur, cœur, œuvre, neuf, neuve, jeune, seul, meuble, peur, beurre, heure.

12. me, te, se, le, ne, je, de, devant, revoir, devoir, recevoir.

gravure, fracture, peureux, vieux, malheureux, professeur, bonheur, coiffeur, théâtre, acteur, ouvreuse, demeurer, déjeuner.

leur sœur est seule, deux œufs, peu de beurre, ma sœur a peur du voleur, Jules brûle du papier, il le lui donne, deux fois neuf font dix-huit.

13. vin, fin, cinq, quinze, jardin, matin, incapable, simple, timbre, importer, impossible, imparfait, main, pain, bain, train, gain, demain, certain, faim, daim, plein, peintre, sein, peinture, ceindre, feindre, Reims.

14. gant, grand, maman, tante, France, janvier, Angleterre, camp, champ, lampe, jambe, chambre, ambassadeur, dent, vent, enfant, enfin, vente, ventre, entendre, temps, temple, membre, trembler, sembler, assembler.

15. on, bon, nom, ton, son, long, montons, bonbon, jambon, pompe, plomb, ombre, nombre, sombre, rompre.

16. un, brun, lundi, chacun, Verdun, Melun, quelqu'un, humble, parfum.

un bon vin blanc, l'enfant mange une orange, elle entre dans la chambre, le chien vient dans le jardin, Henri est content, nous allons en France demain matin, le marin revient avec un grand singe, mon oncle compte son argent.

Consonants

bon, bébé, beurre, bombe, bureau, bouillon, bonbon.
cas, carré, café, col, cour, école, cure, curé, encre, classe, crayon, cri, craie, cravate, chic, sec, grec, lac.
ce, c'est, ceci, cela, ci, cinq, cinéma, cygne, bicyclette, ça, leçon, garçon, français, maçon.
bouche, chou, chef, cheval, chose, chien, mouchoir, cache-cache.
dé, dame, danse, danger, douce, douche, dormir, durant.
face, facile, faible, faire, faveur, fée, chef, œuf, bœuf.

gare, garçon, regardez, gant, gomme, wagon, Gustave, gris, grand.

rouge, page, nage, géographie, Georges, mange, mangeons, gymnastique.

signe, signer, signal, gagner, Allemagne, Bretagne, oignon.

huit, le huitième, le hareng, la Hollande, l'hiver, l'homme, l'histoire.

je, jamais, journal, juin, juillet, joie, jaloux, jalousie, kaki, képi, kilogramme, kilomètre, kiosque.

livre, lampe, balle, cheval, ville, village, mille, tranquille.

maman, maison, méchant, médecin, moment, musique, murmure.

ni, né, nage, nègre, numéro, novembre, noir, nuit, nature.

Paris, papa, pardon, paradis, parapluie, poisson, police, pupitre.

cinq, coq, quinze, cinquante, quand, quatre, quarante, quantité.

rond, rouge, règle, raisin, rire, livre, carte, entre, montre.

salle, sac, six, sortez, son, sous, sœur, sucre, soupe, silence, classe, professeur, assis, tasse, poisson, chaussette, assiette.

chaise, rose, maison, musique, blouse, grise, oiseau, mademoiselle.

toucher, tomber, tourner, sept, huit, thé, théâtre, Théodore.

vin, vont, vent, verre, valable, vieux, Victor, ventre, vivant.

taxe, taxi, luxe, exact, exemple, examen, six, dix, soixante, deuxième, sixième, dixième, dix_enfants, six_hommes, deux_oiseaux.

le yacht, les yeux, la Yougoslavie, royal, loyal, envoyer, payer.

zéro, zoologique, Zouave.

cahier, papier, plumier, encrier, billet, tilleul, bailler, bétail, soleil, oreille, fauteuil, feuille, bouillon.

moi, toi, soi, soif, froid, poisson, pourquoi, oui, pingouin.

lui, pluie, fui, nuit, bruit, huit, cuisine, suivre, cuire.

deux_hommes, deux_enfants, deux garçons, trois_arbres, trois_oranges, trois pommes, cinq_élèves, cinq_encriers, cinq chaises, six_oiseaux, six_enfants, six livres, dix_œillets, dix_avions, dix mouchoirs, les_enfants, les_arbres, les fleurs.

EXERCISES

These exercises should be attempted after the corresponding Fluency Practice has been completely mastered.

Lessons I-III

(a) Answer the following questions both affirmatively and negatively:

Est-ce | le professeur?
la femme de chambre?
un agent de police?
un bon hôtel?
une grande chambre?

(b) Answer affirmatively and negatively, replacing the nouns by pronouns:

Est-ce que | le lit est comfortable?
la chambre est trop petite?
la salle de bains est à droite?
les armoires sont grandes?
les fauteuils sont bons?
le petit garçon entre dans la chambre?
la dame parle anglais?
les dames sont Françaises?
les messieurs sont Américains?
les demoiselles sont Canadiennes?

(c) Answer both affirmatively and negatively:

1. Êtes-vous | Français(e)? 2. Parlez-vous | français?
Anglais(e)? | anglais?
Américain(e)? | italien?
fatigué(e)? | espagnol?

3. Fumez-vous?　　　　Écoutez-vous?
Entrez-vous?　　　　Travaillez-vous beaucoup?
Montez-vous?　　　　Avez-vous une bonne chambre?

(d) Say in the negative:
1. Entrez!
2. Je monte.
3. Écoutez-vous?
4. Parlez français!
5. Elle est petite.
6. Est-il malade?
7. C'est le professeur.
8. Dansez-vous?

(e) Say in French:
1. Come in.
2. Don't come in.
3. Aren't you coming up?
4. I am coming up.
5. Don't speak so fast.
6. You speak French, don't you?
7. A gentlemen is coming in.
8. It is the teacher.
9. He is smoking.
10. It is a large bed.
11. It is very comfortable.
12. Where is the bathroom?
13. There, on the left.
14. These are the rooms.
15. They are small, aren't they?

LESSON IV

(a) Replace the nouns in italics by pronouns:
1. Il met *les vêtements* dans l'armoire.
2. Elle ferme *la porte*.
3. Il ouvre *le livre*.
4. Fermez-vous *la valise*?
5. Prenez-vous *le sac de voyage*?
6. Monte-t-il *les bagages*?
7. Posez *cette valise* devant la fenêtre.
8. Ne prenez pas *cette malle*.
9. Ne fermez pas *cette valise*.
10. Fermez *la porte*.
11. Ouvrez *les fenêtres*.
12. Ne regardez pas *ces livres*.

(b) Answer both affirmatively and negatively, replacing the nouns by pronouns:
1. Aimez-vous le vin (la bière, les oranges, cette couleur-ci, les cigarettes anglaises)?
2. Prenez-vous le parapluie (la valise, le sac de voyage, ces livres-ci, les bagages)?
3. La femme de chambre ouvre-t-elle les fenêtres (la porte, les tiroirs, l'armoire, le sac de voyage)?

(c) Give the negative of:

1. Mettez cette chaise dans le jardin.
2. Elles sont dans le garage.
3. Le parapluie est-il dans l'armoire?
4. Est-il derrière la porte?
5. Prenez ce taxi-là.
6. Prenez-le.
7. Ouvrez-vous la malle?
8. Fermez-vous les fenêtres?
9. Êtes-vous dans le jardin?
10. Ils sont dans l'armoire.
11. J'aime cette couleur.
12. Préférez-vous cette chambre-ci?
13. Prenez-la.
14. Aimez-vous les cigarettes anglaises?
15. Prenez-les.

(d) Say in French:

1. Do you smoke?
2. Don't you speak English?
3. Aren't you American?
4. Isn't she coming up?
5. Have you no smaller room?
6. Here is my luggage.
7. Please take it up.
8. I don't like this room.
9. Put the suitcase on the table.
10. Give me the travelling bag.
11. Don't put it down.

Lesson V

(a) Answer the following questions, replacing the nouns by pronouns:

1. De quelle couleur est votre livre (mon parapluie, votre mouchoir, le chapeau du professeur, la cravate de cet élève)?

2. De quelle couleur sont vos gants (souliers, chaussettes, bas, mouchoirs)?

3. Où est votre livre (parapluie, chapeau, pardessus, chemise)?

4. Où sont vos pantoufles (mouchoirs, chaussettes, bas, cravates)?

5. Avez-vous votre parapluie (mes gants, vos livres, mes souliers)?

(b) Answer both affirmatively and negatively, replacing the nouns by pronouns:
1. Ai-je votre mouchoir (vos gants, votre livre, vos souliers)?
2. Avez-vous mon chapeau (mes pantoufles, mon pantalon, ma valise)?
3. Votre frère a-t-il votre pardessus (ma cravate, votre gilet, mes gants)?

(c) Replace the nouns in italics by pronouns:
1. *Mon pardessus* est noir.
2. *Son chapeau* est brun.
3. *Sa cravate* est rouge.
4. *Ses souliers* sont bleus.
5. *Leurs mouchoirs* sont dans la valise.
6. *Cette robe* est trop courte.
7. Montez *les bagages*.
8. J'ai *le parapluie*.
9. Je prends *les gants*.
10. Elle porte *son manteau vert*.
11. Mettez *les souliers* dans l'armoire.

(d) Replace the words in italics by *son, sa, ses, leur, leurs*:
1. La chambre *de mon frère*.
2. La chambre *de ma sœur*.
3. La chambre *de mes cousins*.
4. Le parapluie *de mon père*.
5. Le parapluie *de ma mère*.
6. La maison *de mes grands-parents*.
7. Les robes *de ma tante*.
8. Les enfants *de mon oncle*.

(e) Say in French:
1. My brown hat is in the wardrobe.
2. Where is your umbrella?
3. It is behind that chair.
4. Is his tie grey or green?
5. Is her hat blue or black?
6. Are these your gloves?
7. Where are my handkerchiefs?
8. Aren't they on the chest of drawers?
9. Look! Here they are.
10. Their shoes are in front of the door.

Lesson VI

(a) Answer both affirmatively and negatively:

    1. Mangez-vous du fromage (de la viande, des sardines)?

    2. Avez-vous du pain (de la viande, des biscottes, de l'eau)?

    3. Votre sœur a-t-elle du beurre (de la salade, des légumes)?

(b) Repeat the above questions and in your answers replace all nouns by pronouns.

(c) Answer the following questions, replacing the nouns by pronouns: Combien avez-vous de chapeaux (robes, cravates, mouchoirs, livres français)?

(d) Read these numbers:

    7, 11, 13, 15, 12, 14, 16, 18, 23, 34, 45, 54, 29, 38, 49, 57.

(e) Say in French:

    1. What time is lunch?

    2. What is there for dinner?

    3. What is the time now?

    4. Do you like rusks?

    5. Do you take sugar?

    6. How many lumps do you take?

    7. Is there any milk?

    8. Please bring sugar and cream.

    9. Haven't they any rolls?

    10. There is no butter on the table.

Lesson VII

(a) Answer both affirmatively and negatively, replacing the nouns by pronouns:

| Est-ce que | les messieurs
les dames | dansent?
chantent?
travaillent?
jouent?
montent? |

(b) Insert the missing endings:

    1. Nous all—— au cinéma ce soir.

    2. Mes parents travers—— la rue.

3. Elle travaill—— jusqu'à cinq heures.
4. Je n'aim—— pas la bière.
5. Ven—— vous avec moi?
6. Il parl—— bien le français.
7. Elles ne chant—— pas.

(c) Answer both affirmatively and negatively:
  1. Venez-vous du théâtre?
  2. Allez-vous au cinéma?
  3. Ai-je votre livre?
  4. Avez-vous mon chapeau?
  5. Écoutez-vous?
  6. Est-ce la valise de votre sœur?
  7. Est-ce que ce sont les gants de votre frère?

(d) Say in French:
  1. Are you going to sing?
  2. He is going to play.
  3. They are going to dance.
  4. Where are you going?
  5. I am going to the casino.
  6. Where are you coming from?
  7. I am coming from the hotel.
  8. Aren't they playing?
  9. What time does he come from the office?
  10. She is not coming from the station.

(e) Quelle heure est-il?
  6.15, 7.30, 8.45, 9.50, 10.05, 11.40, 12.10, 12.30, 1.55, 2.25.

LESSON VIII

(a) Say in the future:
  1. Il prend le petit déjeuner à 8 heures.
  2. Je n'ai pas assez de sucre.
  3. Elles mangent du pain?
  4. Je suis fatigué.
  5. Nous allons en France.
  6. Elles sont en Écosse.
  7. Ils ont faim.
  8. Tu as bien des livres.

(*b*) Answer these questions:

1. Mangez-vous beaucoup de viande?
2. Buvez-vous de la bière?
3. Votre sœur boit-elle du vin?
4. Prenez-vous du café après le dîner?
5. Prendrez-vous du sucre?
6. Irez-vous en France cette année?
7. Où serez-vous ce soir?
8. Votre frère viendra-t-il ici demain?
9. Quand aurez-vous vos vacances?
10. Avez-vous soif?

(*c*) Say in French:

1. Will you take soup?
2. What fish will there be?
3. You don't eat enough vegetables.
4. Don't eat too much meat.
5. What will you drink?
6. Does she drink cocoa?
7. I shall eat a mushroom omelette.
8. My wife will take some stewed fruit.
9. Where will you go this year?
10. We shall be in Switzerland in a fortnight from to-day.

LESSON IX

(*a*) Read these numbers:

14, 25, 47, 51, 62, 72, 83, 94, 15, 65, 75, 87, 98.

(*b*) Add one of the following adjectives to each of the nouns (making it feminine or plural where necessary):

bon, mauvais, beau, jeune, vieux, nouveau, blanc, noir, français, long.

1. idée	6. souliers
2. statue	7. femme
3. château	8. journal
4. ville	9. rue
5. cheval	10. habitude

(c) Say in French:

1. Is there a bus stop near here?
2. Which bus must I take to go to the station?
3. What street is this?
4. Do I have to get off here?
5. You cannot go there by bus.
6. Can I take the Underground?
7. Is it very far from here?
8. There is an Underground station at the end of the street.
9. It is near the museum.
10. You can cross the road now.

LESSON X

(a) Answer the questions on page 58 both affirmatively and negatively.

(b) Replace the nouns in italics by pronouns:

1. Pourquoi regardez-vous *cette femme?*
2. Achèterez-vous *ces fleurs?*
3. J'écris *à mon ami.*
4. Ne parlez pas *à ces enfants.*
5. Nous attendons *l'autobus.*
6. Il envoie un cadeau *à sa fiancée.*
7. Elle offre sa place *au vieux monsieur.*
8. Donnerez-vous un pourboire *à la femme de chambre?*

(c) Say in French:

1. What a beautiful picture!
2. Will you buy it?
3. Will he sell it?
4. We are sending her a postcard.
5. Don't you want to write to her?
6. I shall see her to-night.
7. Don't tell her that.
9. Will you speak to them?
9. Here is the manager. Let's ask him.
10. I do not know how much money to give them.

109

(*a*) Read the following dates:
2/5/1940,   6/8/1851,   21/3/1903,   18/4/1916,   30/6/1927,
11/7/1954,   12/4/1776,   31/1/1899.

(*b*) Answer the following questions:
1. Quel jour de la semaine est-ce?
2. Quel jour sera-ce demain?
3. Quelle est la date d'aujourd'hui?
4. Êtes-vous né en 1952?
5. Quel est le premier mois de l'année?
6. Est-ce que vous faites de la gymnastique chaque matin?
7. Viendrez-vous ici demain?
8. Que ferez-vous demain soir?
9. Lisez-vous beaucoup de romans?
10. Sera-ce dimanche demain?

(*c*) Say in French:
1. He has just arrived.
2. Where are you?
3. What are you doing?
4. Where are they?
5. What are they doing?
6. What are they saying?
7. What time will the train leave?
8. Have they any rooms?
9. They haven't any.
10. Will you give me the pleasure of your company at lunch?

Lesson XII

(*a*) Replace the nouns in italics by pronouns:
1. Prenez *le cahier*.
2. Apportez *la viande*.
3. Montrez *les billets*.
4. Achetez *les allumettes*.
5. Montrez *votre stylo à ce monsieur*.
6. Apportez *ces fleurs à Mademoiselle Lucienne*.

7. Ne montrez pas *cette lettre à votre femme.*
8. Il vendra *son automobile à mon ami Gaston.*
9. J'enverrai *ce paquet à ma mère.*
10. Ils donneront *des cadeaux à leurs enfants.*
11. Que direz-vous *à votre sœur?*
12. Rendrez-vous *les livres à votre professeur?*

(*b*) Say the above sentences in the negative.

(*c*) Say the sentences under (*a*) in the negative, replacing all nouns by pronouns.

(*d*) Reply both affirmatively and negatively, replacing the nouns by pronouns:

1. Est-ce que je vous donne | mon chapeau?
   ma cravate?
   mes souliers?

2. Me donnez-vous | votre parapluie?
   votre montre?
   vos gants?

3. Enverrez-vous ces fleurs | à votre oncle?
   à ma tante?
   à vos cousines?

(*e*) Say in French:
1. Why don't you show them to her?
2. He will sell it (the car) to us.
3. Are there any peaches?
4. No, there aren't any.
5. Bring it (the cup) to her.
6. Send them to him.
7. Give it (the book) back to her.
8. Will you not show them (the snapshots) to me?
9. Will you not give us any?
10. Open it (the door).
11. Don't shut them (the windows).
12. She lends it (the umbrella) to you.
13. Let us sell it (the car) to him.

(*a*) Answer the questions on pages 73 and 74 both affirmatively and negatively.

(*b*) Answer the following questions:
1. M'avez-vous vu hier?
2. Avez-vous mangé des œufs ce matin?
3. Qu'avez-vous bu?
4. Avez-vous pris un bain?
5. Avez-vous écrit à vos amis?
6. Avez-vous parlé français avant la leçon?
7. Votre cousin vous a-t-il écrit?
8. Mon frère vous a-t-il prêté son livre?
9. Où avez-vous été hier soir?
10. Qu'est-ce que vous avez fait?
11. Avez-vous vu Monsieur Duval?
12. Vos amis ont-ils vendu leur maison?
13. Avez-vous lu le journal?
14. Vos sœurs ont-elles bien dormi?
15. Avez-vous été au théâtre hier soir?

(*c*) Repeat the following sentences in the *Passe Composé*:
1. Elle lit tous les journaux.
2. Ils jouent aux cartes tous les soirs.
3. Je prends du café noir.
4. Nous buvons du vin blanc.
5. Où mettez-vous la valise?
6. Dort-il?
7. Ne fait-il pas sa promenade du matin?
8. Ne mange-t-elle pas?
9. Ils ont soif.

(*a*) Answer the questions on page 78 both affirmatively and negatively.

(*b*) Answer the following questions:
1. Allez-vous souvent au théâtre?
2. Y êtes-vous allé hier soir?

3. Y irez-vous demain?
4 A quelle heure êtes-vous venu ici?
5. Votre sœur est-elle venue avec vous?
6. A quelle heure êtes-vous sorti ce matin?
7. Avez-vous été à Paris?
8. Êtes-vous arrivé à la Gare du Nord?
9. Combien de jours y êtes-vous resté?
10. Voudriez-vous aller en France la semaine prochaine?
11. Iriez-vous si vous n'aviez pas d'argent?
12. Qu'est-ce que vous feriez si vous aviez beaucoup d'argent?

(*c*) Say in French:
1. Don't go there.
2. I went there last month.
3. I stayed there three weeks.
4. I came back on August 15th.
5. We left on July 23rd.
6. Hasn't she come back yet?
7. At what time did the train arrive?
8. Where have you been?
9. I went to the cinema.
10. What did you see?
11. Have you had your dinner?
12. What did you eat?
13. What would you do if I gave you the money?
14. Would you go there if she was not there?
15. I should like to see her.

(*d*) Say the *Imparfait, Passé Composé, Futur* and *Conditionnel* of:

1. Il travaille.	5. Ils ont faim.
2. Nous sortons.	6. Je leur écris.
3. Je suis fatigué.	7. Elle me le dit.
4. Venez-vous?	8. Où va-t-il?

LESSON XV

(*a*) Answer the following questions:
1. À quelle heure vous réveillez-vous?
2. Est-ce que vous vous levez aussitôt que vous vous réveillez?

3. À quelle heure votre frère se lève-t-il?
4. Combien d'heures avez-vous dormi?
5. Comment vous appelez-vous?
6. Comment s'appelle votre sœur?
7. Ce livre est-il à vous?
8. À quelle heure êtes-vous sorti ce matin?
9. Avez-vous mis votre pardessus?

(b) Say in French:
1. Wake up.
2. Don't get up yet.
3. Our friend is washing.
4. Your father is shaving.
5. Don't forget to brush your hair.
6. Is she getting dressed?
7. What time does he go to bed?
8. I went out with them.
9. Don't leave without him.
10. Have a good time.

(c) Read the following numbers:
64, 74, 85, 95, 23, 32, 54, 45, 71, 92, 105, 216, 377, 893, 1567, 3459.

Lesson XVI

(a) Repeat the sentences in Exercise VIII (a), page 107, in the *Passé Composé*.

(b) Answer the questions on page 87 both affirmatively and negatively.

(c) Say in French:
1. What time did you get up?
2. Let us go for a walk in the park.
3. The open air will do you good.
4. It would do me good if I had a warm coat.
5. It is so cold.
6. I caught a cold.
7. I have a headache and a sore throat.
8. I am sorry to hear it.

9. What did you do last night?
10. We went to the theatre.
11. What did you see?
12. Did you have a good time?

(*d*) Answer the following questions:

1. Est-ce qu'il fait du soleil aujourd'hui?
2. A-t-il fait beau hier?
3. Pleut-il maintenant?
4. A-t-il plu ce matin?
5. Quel temps a-t-il fait hier?
6. Fait-il froid aujourd'hui?
7. Fait-il chaud en hiver?
8. Est-ce qu'il pleut souvent en été?
9. Est-ce qu'il neige beaucoup en hiver?
10. Où passez-vous vos vacances?

(*e*) Give the *Passé Composé, Imparfait, Futur* and *Conditionnel* corresponding to:

1. Il sort.
2. Elle met son chapeau.
3. Je m'endors.
4. Avez-vous mal au dents?
5. Ils sont malades.
6. Elle s'habille.
7. Je vais au cinéma.
8. Nous prenons du café.
9. Elles viennent.
10. Il ne boit pas de vin.

INDEX

Numbers refer to pages; those in brackets denote the relevant Fluency Practice or Explanations section.